22 Boyfriends to Happiness

My Story

& The Seven Secrets on how to find True Love

Catherine Buchan

British Library Cataloguing-in-Publication Data
A catalogue record for this book is available from the
British Library

First Published in the United Kingdom in 2008
Cover design by Pentacorbig
Printed and bound by Anthony Rowe Ltd, Chippenham, Wiltshire

www.catherinebuchan.com
ISBN: 978-0-9557317-0-9

Table of Contents

Acknowledgements...v

Preface...vii

PART ONE My Story 1

Chapter 1 Ben – my first love..3

Chapter 2 Anthony – my half Latin love.......................................11

Chapter 3 The return of Anthony..19

Chapter 4 Tim – my boss..29

Chapter 5 Still looking for love in the wrong place....................37

Chapter 6 John – the vegetarian...51

Chapter 7 Harry – the guy with the Porsche...............................59

Chapter 8 The return of John...65

Chapter 9 Beginning to look for love in the right place.............73

Chapter 10 Alex – almost The One...83

Chapter 11 Single and content, eventually..................................95

Chapter 12 Mark – The One..105

PART TWO The Seven Secrets on How to Find True
Love 117

Introduction...119

Secret 1 Know Yourself..127

Secret 2 Love yourself..141

Secret 3 Be true to yourself...155

Secret 4 Do what makes your heart sing...................................169

Secret 5 Know what you want and ask for it..............................181

Secret 6 Become The One..193

Secret 7 Let go...203

Conclusion...215

Bibliography and further reading..217

Other resources...220

About the author...222

Acknowledgements

My heartfelt thanks to: my parents Pam and Ray Parry for their support; my brother James Parry for the inspired title; to Sarah O'Mahoney, Laurika Bretherton, Eithne Farry and Susie Lea for reading my first draft and for their honest and valuable feedback; to Alex Howard, Helen O'Mahoney and Viv Knowland for their continual enthusiasm and encouragement of this book and my work; to Kirandeep Kaur Chodha for allowing me to include her moving poem; to Paul Lamb at Leeds library for our conversations during my writing breaks; to Dr Doreen Virtue and Steven Falmer for being such great teachers and to my fellow PSTTP community members for their encouragement and words of wisdom along the way.

I would like to thank the following for assisting me greatly with the process of granting permission to quote from their publications: Shari Claire, Global 13 Publications; Ali Nightingale, Hay House Publishing; Annemarie Fearnley, Piatkus Books; Catherine Trippett, The Random House Group and to Mike George. My thanks also go to Margaret Aherne, my copy-editor, for her professionalism, support and assistance during the process.

I would like to express my deepest gratitude to my soulmate, husband and best friend Mark Buchan for his endless support, patience and encouragement throughout the writing of this book. I'd like to thank him for believing in the message and in me, and for ensuring that the book was published. Thanks for cooking me all those wonderful meals, for sharing the domestics, for your jokes, for your great coaching and everything else too. You really are my earth angel.

Finally, I am eternally grateful to the Universe for continuously illuminating the path and supporting me in so many wonderful ways throughout this journey, and for showing me the way to true love.

Preface

Are you without a partner? Do you feel lonely and un-happy? Would you like to stop being unhappily single? Or are you in a relationship but unsure if your partner is 'The One' or not? Do you believe that true love exists but you haven't found it yet? Would you like to experience true love? Would you like to find out how to become happier? If you answered 'Yes' to any of these questions, this is the book for you.

This book reveals an effective way of finding true love that some might consider unconventional. This method is effective because its foundation lies in timeless fundamental truths, also known as universal laws or principles, such as the Universal Law of Attraction. There is a body of literature to support the power of these timeless fundamental truths, detailing numerous examples of how people have benefited from them in many areas of their lives. However, what is unique about this book is that it takes these inter-related principles and focuses on the aspects which specifically en-hance the process of finding true love.

What is unconventional about the method described in this book is that it involves what I call the 'Seven Secrets'. Although I do not suggest that the Seven Secrets are the only answer to finding true love, I tried for many years searching for love in more conventional ways. This only led me further away from true love and deepened my unhappiness. In contrast, this less conventional method – which requires us to develop with ourselves the relationship we seek with another, rather than seek love solely outside of ourselves – resulted in my finding true love and happiness and a life that I had previously only dreamt about.

This book is divided into two parts. Part One is an open and candid account of my own challenging search for true love, from blindly searching outside of myself for solutions to my loneliness and unhappiness, to using the less conventional methods which led me to discover the wisdom of the Seven Secrets.

I believe this book stands out from other useful self-help books on love and relationships because I have bared my soul in this way, sharing my own experiences, from the amusing ones to those that were confusing, embarrassing, painful and occasionally even humiliating. For me, this was essential in order to illustrate the lessons that I learnt and how I learnt them. It also demonstrates that if I have been able to find true love using the Seven Secrets, considering how I used to feel about myself and all the ways I searched for love in the past, then others can too!

Part Two reveals the Seven Secrets on how to find true love, an unconventional but easy-to-follow guide, which you can use to apply the Seven Secrets in your own life in order to find true love and The One. This section also includes a simple checklist to help you to recognise The One and a true love relationship quickly and easily.

In reading my story and working through the Seven Secrets you will have the opportunity to become more self-aware, more self-empowered, more 'attractive' and have more fun. You will also become clearer about what you want and how to get it. In the process you will discover the true love that you have been searching for all along.

In case you are thinking that you might have to have 22 boyfriends (or girlfriends) before you can find true love, let me reassure you that it isn't necessary! You may also observe that the men included in my story were not all 'boyfriends' technically. Some were just encounters of varying degrees. Nevertheless, I believe it's what I learnt from each experience that's important, as it is for us all, and you will notice that this is demonstrated in the pages that follow.

The experiences described are all true as far as my memory and journals serve me. Only the names have been changed to protect people's privacy. I believe that the actual identity of the people is irrelevant compared to the lessons learnt.

Finally, there is not one single book that supplies all the answers for everyone, as I discovered on my own journey to true love. There will be some points in the story and the Seven Secrets that you relate to and others that you may not. So, I encourage you to take on board only that which you do relate to and develop from there.

I wish you all the love and happiness that you dream of.

Blessings

Catherine Buchan

PART ONE

My Story

CHAPTER 1

Ben – my first love

A lonely start

If I had to use a single word to describe my childhood, I would say it was lonely. Being the only child of busy parents I would often spend hours alone in my room amusing myself. When I wasn't playing with my dolls or talking to my teddy bears, I buried my head in books. I loved escaping in my mind to the happy world of the all-girl boarding schools Enid Blyton wrote about, imagining what it would be like to have friends around me all the time and to never feel alone.

I also loved fairytales with their happy-ever-after endings. I used to fantasise about getting married one day. I imagined wearing the beautiful white dress, having the big church wedding and, of course, my own handsome prince. During these early years I experienced bullying too. I felt even more isolated as a result. Fantasising about romantic love and a happier future helped me cope with the deep feelings of loneliness and the bullying I endured.

When I was 11, my brother James was born. For years I'd wanted a sibling. 'Now I won't be lonely any more', I thought to myself. I was wrong. My parents became even busier looking after him and he was too young to be company for me. Then, suddenly, puberty arrived and my life got even worse. The more my body changed, the uglier and less confident I felt. How I wished a fairy godmother would appear in my life, wave a magic wand and give me a prettier face, bigger boobs, longer hair and a new wardrobe!

Despite the uncontrollable changes I was experiencing thanks to puberty, I continued to believe it was only a matter of time, of growing up, before my fantasy would become a reality and I'd find true love and happiness. By the time I was 17, though, my so-called relationships weren't lasting any longer than four weeks. I was already beginning to wonder if The One would ever turn up.

However, things started to change when I got a part-time job in a local store. I made many new friends, both male and female, and established a good social life. I began to feel popular and it boosted my self-esteem. I was also beginning to fall for someone. His name was Ben. He was a full-time employee and my supervisor.

Ben was not particularly tall, but he was dark and handsome. He was working his way up through the ranks in retail management. He wore a suit to work and had an air of authority about him. I thought he seemed strong and power-ful. He was also warm and friendly and had a lovely smile. He captured my heart.

Getting together

One day, I plucked up the courage to confide in a close friend of mine who worked at the store and knew Ben well. She found out for me that he was single, and agreed to invite him to the pub with us after work, along with a few other colleagues. He accepted.

I couldn't wait for work to end. My friend and I set off to the pub. Once there, I bought myself a drink to calm my nerves. Ben joined us shortly afterwards, looking very casual in jeans and a t-shirt. My heart somersaulted when I saw him. Ben didn't do flirting so I spent the evening trying to work out if he was attracted to me or not. I was worried it was going to be another experience of unrequited love, something I would have to force myself to get over. However, as other people started to drift home, he seemed in no hurry to leave.

Ben, who I'd discovered lived only a five-minute drive away from me, eventually offered me a lift home. I thought he was doing it to be nice and because we lived so near each other. We pulled up outside my house and Ben got out and walked me to my door. We were standing very close together, and as I thanked him for giving me a lift home he pulled me towards him and kissed me. Romantic thoughts filled my Libran head, and in that moment I fell in love for the first time. He asked me out. We were officially dating. It seemed almost too good to be true.

Shortly afterwards, I introduced Ben to my family. My whole family loved him, especially my Mum. He was just the sort of guy she'd been hoping I'd bring home: handsome, polite, respectable and with good career prospects. Definitely marriage material!

I was relieved to find that Ben's family appeared to like me too, even permitting me to stay over at their house at weekends, on the condition that I slept in the spare room. We made the most of having the house to ourselves while they were at church on Sunday mornings.

Losing my virginity

As with most teenagers, the state of my love-life prior to dating Ben had been far from my only issue. I had also lost belief in myself, particularly in terms of my intelligence. So, rather than undertake a three-year degree at university, I had chosen to study a course-work based, two-year diploma at polytechnic and had been accepted on a course in Essex, which was a few hours drive from home . I was taking a year out, doing a full-time office job, in addition to working evenings and Saturdays at the store. My goal was to save enough money to support myself through the diploma course. I had one year to achieve my financial goal. I also had a year to achieve a goal of a different kind.

At 18 years old I was still a virgin – a result of personal choice and commitment to myself rather than lack of opportunity. Nevertheless, I did want to lose my virginity before I went off to polytechnic. I was afraid of people making fun of me if I was still a virgin. I didn't want to end up isolated and lonely again. After eight months of dating Ben, I was convinced we were in love and felt ready to make love to him. Wanting to ensure we would be alone, I arranged for us to stay at my Gran's caravan in Dorset for a few days. It wasn't what you would call a romantic venue, and as it was March I knew it would be freezing cold at night, but it was free and at least we'd have some privacy.

Losing my virginity had been something I had often thought about – almost as much as getting married. I used to wonder what exactly you're meant to do (aside from the obvious!), what it feels like and what happens afterwards. I believed losing my virginity would help me feel like a 'real woman'. I also hoped it would cause people to treat me differently, listen to me and respect me more as a result, especially my parents. I had built it up to be a big milestone in my life and consequently, as I lay in bed with Ben in the icy cold caravan, I felt overwhelmed by anxiety. We did eventually make love. It wasn't an earth-shattering experience, but we found we got better at it with practice!

All too soon our time at the caravan was over and we returned to reality, making do with brief moments of intimacy on Sunday mornings once more. The lack of private moments didn't harm our relationship, though, and we plodded along without any major issues in the months prior to my move to Essex. It was all very nice.

Being with Ben, I felt more confident and I enjoyed being part of a couple. It helped me to feel accepted, to feel that I belonged. I believed it was true love. When I spent four weeks in France brushing up on my French I missed Ben physically as well as emotionally, which further convinced me it was true love. A few days before I moved to polytechnic, Ben even talked about wanting to marry me if we were still together when I finished my two-year course. I suspected he was The One. I believed we'd be together forever.

Spreading my wings

My Mum and Dad were taking me to the Halls of Residence in Essex on Sunday. I knew I wouldn't be able to cope emotionally if Ben took me. It would be too heart-wrenching.

After nearly two hours on the road, we reached our destination. 'Halls' turned out to be a site consisting of around ten purpose-built houses. Each house was to be shared by five males and five females. It would be my home for the first year of the course. On arrival, I was given the keys and shown to my room. It took a while to unload all my belongings. When we'd finished, my parents said goodbye and left. I was all alone in my new room. The giant step I had taken hit me. I broke down in tears. Despite being 19 years old, desperate to leave home and experience freedom, I felt lonely and afraid. I missed Ben, my friends and all the familiar comforts of home. Had I made a mistake?

Following a sleepless night, I nervously made my way to the introductory class the next morning. As I sat in the classroom surrounded by strangers, I ached again for the familiarity and security of Ben. A few minutes later, though, my attention was drawn to the opposite side of the room.

There, standing out from the crowd, was an incredibly gorgeous, tall, blond, suntanned guy named Anthony. Feelings of guilt temporarily washed over me. What was happening to me? 'I'm going out with Ben. I love him', I reminded myself as I pushed the dangerous thoughts to the back of my mind and concentrated on settling into my new life at polytechnic.

Moving apart

If it was true love, though, why was it that, during that first month in Essex, when Ben visited me and wanted to be alone with me, to wine and dine me rather than go to the student bar and socialise with my new friends, did I begin to resent him? If this was true love, why did I feel stifled and trapped? Why did I now want more than 'nice'?

Throughout my life, I had always strived to be good and to do the right thing. I had conformed rigidly throughout my childhood and teens. I was fed up with being a 'good girl' and with other people perceiving me as such too. Although life at polytechnic was freeing in many ways as I had no-one checking up on me, wanting to know where I was going, who I was going with, what I'd be doing and when I'd be back, I wasn't completely happy. I wasn't interested in doing drugs, but I did want to shake off my square image. Like the character Sandy in 'Grease', I wanted to be transformed into an alluring, sexy and liberated woman.

In addition, absence wasn't making my heart grow fonder. It was making it look elsewhere! Not only was I thinking more about Anthony, whom fate had decided I would be living with in the Halls of Residence, but I had also became romantically involved on a very casual basis with another guy, Zac, who also had a partner back home. We weren't deeply interested in each other – we both just wanted some hugs, kisses and affection. I didn't feel guilty about it. I convinced myself that as long as I didn't sleep with Zac, I wasn't really being unfaithful.

Consequently, Ben started to feel like a chain around my neck, keeping me anchored in my restricted past. I still had strong feelings for him but they were mixed with feelings of resentment and suppressed anger. It was like a double-edged sword, made worse by my desperate need to feel love and affection on a daily basis.

By the time the Christmas holidays arrived and I returned home, I knew I did not feel the same love for Ben that I had before I had gone to Essex, and yet I could not bring myself to end our relationship. But events took an unexpected turn.

At the beginning of the holidays, Ben and I were sitting in my bedroom at my parents' house one night. Out of the blue, he said 'we could do with a break'. He didn't mean a trip away together. I felt physically sick and struggled to breathe. I escaped from the room and had a drink in an attempt to calm myself down. I tried to take in what he had said. Ben had been thinking the unthinkable, of dumping me. My heart and mind were racing. I felt shocked and afraid. What would I do without his love?

Feeling a little calmer, I went back up to my bedroom. We continued to talk. Ben admitted it had only been a suggestion as we hadn't been getting on too well. In the end, neither of us felt ready to finish it.

The break-up

I hadn't been back at polytechnic for long when I realised I could no longer deny the truth, to myself or to Ben. The discomfort of living a lie had become greater than the fear of being without his love. I ended the relationship. He accepted the news reasonably well. He even said he could remain friends with me. I was very surprised. It was a different story a few weeks later.

While we were dating, Ben and I had arranged to go to the store's 'dinner and dance' in January. We had booked a double room at the hotel for the night. Following the break-up, Ben said we should still go to the event together. He told me he was still happy for us to share the hotel room (and bed) for the night as we were friends. I had my doubts, but pushed them to the back of my mind. Neither of us had been open with our colleagues about the break-up. Ben didn't want any questions about his private life and I feared being thought badly of by the other employees as he was very popular. So it suited us both to pretend to be together for one last night.

That night we put on our masks of pretence. Through-out the event we did our best to act as though we were still together. It felt very strange and quite uncomfortable. At the end of the evening we went back to our room. I wanted to go to sleep. Ben was confused. He thought that by agreeing to go to the event with him, and share a bed, I wanted us to get back together. I reiterated it was over between us. He broke down. Seeing him suffer was awful. He was a really nice guy and I continued to care about him. I had not meant to hurt him, but I could see that I had and I felt so guilty. It was a very long night.

The next morning, I left the hotel as soon as I could and retreated to the safety of my polytechnic world. Ben had not been The One for me after all. Perhaps I would find happiness in the arms of someone else – possibly even the gorgeous Anthony

CHAPTER 2

Anthony – my half Latin love

Good friends

I was so happy to see Anthony again. Even though it was January, he looked suntanned as usual. He had told me at the start of the first term that he was half English and half Spanish, and that his lovely golden suntan was due to the fact that he lived in the Canary Islands when he wasn't at polytechnic. As the weeks had passed, it had become clear to my housemates and me which half of Anthony was English and which was Spanish, as he often had a woman (usually not his steady girlfriend Lisa, who lived in another part of the country) in his room and it hadn't sounded as though they were in there studying! With his good looks and charisma I wasn't surprised he was so popular with women.

Nevertheless, Anthony didn't seem to have many real friends. I felt sad about that. The more I had got to know him, the more I felt he was a genuinely great guy underneath all his bravado. It seemed to me that his behaviour was really a cry for help, a plea to be loved. Sometimes, I had imagined myself to be the person to give him that love. I wanted to make him happy. The fact that he was gorgeous and irresistibly sexy made it even more tempting. But, he had a steady girlfriend.

A week or so later, though, as luck would have it, Anthony told me he was no longer dating Lisa. He had tired of their constant arguing. I knew their relationship had been a volatile one, but I never thought they would actually break up. Anthony and I were now firm friends and getting on better than ever. He was being really supportive, too, after my own relationship break-up. Yet, even though we flirted with each other, I dared not hope for anything more. He seemed to have been with so many sexy women. What would he ever see in me? I couldn't compete. Not only that, but it had felt safe for me to flirt with Anthony when I had been going out with Ben. It had been harmless. Now, though, I knew I could get hurt if I got carried away with my romantic fantasy. I had to be careful.

More than just good friends

Later that month, Anthony and I were sitting in our communal kitchen across the table from one another one night. Suddenly our eyes met. We sat looking intensely at each other. Neither of us pulled away. We ignored everything going on around us: the music, the cooking, the questions from the other housemates. Everything. We were locked in our own secret world. I felt Anthony's eyes penetrating me. It felt as though he could see through to my very core. I'd never felt such chemistry with anyone before. It was electric. I didn't want it to end.

Without altering his gaze, Anthony broke our silence. He asked me to go to the student bar with him. Was it actually a date, though, or just a drink with a friend he was flirting heavily with? I wasn't sure. I didn't want to risk being hurt or looking foolish, so I tried to act nonchalantly as we made the fifteen-minute walk to the bar.

Following a few drinks and more teasing and flirting, Anthony took me by the hand and led me outside. He pushed me gently up against the wall. He leaned into me and kissed me. Incredible feelings flooded my body. I felt like I was on fire. It was amazing. Did Anthony really want more than friendship? Was this actually happening to me?

We kissed passionately again. Suddenly, Anthony wanted to leave and quickly. We walked back to Halls. He invited me up to his room. I hesitated. A part of me wanted to seize this golden opportunity. The fact that he, the gorgeous Anthony, found me desirable made me feel so good. But I was afraid of being just another notch on what I suspected was a well-worn bedpost. I was strong and agreed to go back to his room on the condition that we didn't make love. He accepted my decision, although it didn't stop him trying to persuade me to change my mind!

The passion and electricity flowing between us soon became too much for me. I was starting to surrender to his charms. I tore myself away and retreated to my own room. The internal conflict I was battling with, combined with my racing heart, made it virtually impossible for me to sleep. I desperately wanted Anthony to make love to me but I really didn't want to be a one-night stand. Word usually spread quickly around Halls. I was afraid of what other people might think and say about me, especially Zac, if I slept with Anthony. I was also frightened of ruining any chance I might have of developing a real relationship with him. What was I getting myself into?

The following night Anthony asked me up to his room again. Wow. He was still interested in me. It was such an incredibly tempting offer. How could I refuse? I doubted I could resist his persuasive charms a second night. 'What the hell. You're only young once', I thought to myself as I accepted his invitation. The second he kissed me, I felt the full force of the passion flooding through me. It was intoxicating. I allowed my resolve of the previous night to cave in. We made love. I felt the earth move – a lot! I was hooked. I felt so energised and alive. Anthony had unlocked a deep passion in me. However, I was determined only to be 'in lust' with him. I was just going to have some fun and shower him with the love I believed he needed. But I hadn't planned for the feelings he evoked in me becoming so addictive. His attention and affection quickly became my cocaine. I needed regular fixes.

After we had been sleeping together for several weeks it dawned on me that all Anthony wanted to do with me was have sex. I couldn't understand it. I'd replaced his girlfriend, hadn't I? Why hadn't he asked me out on a proper date? Was he ashamed to be seen out with me? Was I not good enough? My self-esteem nose-dived. I wanted to ask him about it, but I was too afraid. I was afraid of hearing the truth and of being rejected. It wasn't until my friend convinced me that if Anthony really cared for me he would take me on a proper date that I plucked up the courage to question him about it. It didn't matter to me why it had taken him so long to ask me on a date, as long as he wanted to be with me in public. Thankfully, he did.

One night, shortly after our first proper date, Lisa turned up at Halls in a bit of a state. Anthony took her up to his bedroom where they proceeded to argue so loudly we could all hear what was going on. After a while, Lisa knocked on the door of my room and asked to speak to me. She gave me a tearful hug, told me to look after Anthony and then left. What did she mean? It was as though they'd only just broken up. I was confused and extremely anxious. Anthony confessed he had still been seeing Lisa behind my back. He had only just ended it. He said he had felt unable to end their relationship until now because, during his previous attempts, Lisa had got very drunk and distraught. I struggled to take in what he was saying. But I was so 'in lust' and dependent on him that I buried my true thoughts and feelings and did my best to forget about the experience.

The disappearance

The months passed and all was well in our relationship. We reached the end of the first year of the diploma. The day of the results of the coursework arrived: to my relief, I discovered I had passed. I felt very happy and went to find Anthony to share my good news. He told me he had failed. It meant he wouldn't be able to go on to the second year. He was livid.

Out of the blue, it seemed Anthony would be going back to the Canary Islands – for good. I was devastated. My world was turned upside down. Anthony was so furious about the whole thing that I didn't dare ask him what it meant in terms of our relationship. I was too afraid to ask if he would consider staying in England to be with me, which is what I secretly wished for. Instead, I quietly packed up my belongings and moved back to my parents' house for the summer.

I spent the holidays waiting in hope for Anthony to contact me. I felt in limbo emotionally, and embarrassed when anyone asked me how my romance was going. I didn't know what to say. I felt stupid not knowing and I felt rejected. I missed him so much but I had to start to face the fact that I would be going back to polytechnic unhappily single.

At the end of the holidays, I had very mixed feelings about returning to Essex. On the one hand I was desperate to experience freedom again, to see my friends and achieve the diploma. On the other, I was afraid of being there without

Anthony. He had been such a major part of my polytechnic life. It wouldn't be the same without him.

Anthony reappears

Just before the start of the second year, I was in my new student house one night when my housemate told me she'd heard that Anthony had been given permission to re-take the first year of the diploma. She also said that someone had seen Anthony in town that week. I didn't know what to make of it all. I was excited to think that he might have been given another chance and that we could be together again. I also felt incredibly hurt. He was supposed to be my boyfriend. I had given him my heart. Why hadn't he called me himself to tell me the news? Why hadn't he rushed to see me as soon as he returned to Essex? Later that night, I had the opportunity to find out when he turned up on my doorstep.

I felt myself shaking as I led him up to my room. He was his usual charming self and behaved as though nothing was wrong. I had expected him to say he was sorry he hadn't called. I had also hoped he would say he hadn't stopped thinking about me for the whole of the summer holidays. I heard nothing of the sort. I felt angry for a brief moment. Then I realised how desperately I wanted to be with him and how relieved I was that he was sitting in my bedroom, appearing to want to continue dating me. I didn't want to jeopardise our future. So, as Anthony gave me some reasons why he had acted the way he had, I chose to accept them. All I wanted was to be with him and make love again. Once more, I buried my thoughts and feelings and we went to bed.

Five months later, we celebrated our one-year anniversary. Anthony said he was taking me away for the day to celebrate. It was a grey, drizzly day but the sun was shining in my heart as I congratulated myself on managing to stay with Anthony for one whole year. I was definitely not another notch on his bedpost now. I had become his steady girlfriend. I had even met his Mum. I felt very good about myself. Surely I was good enough after all if I was able to attract (and 'keep') someone as wonderful as him. Everything was perfect.

My first heartbreak

One week later, I arrived on campus following a rare night in my own place to see Anthony standing on the path outside one of the classrooms. It seemed he was waiting for me. Even after a year of dating, my heart leapt every time I saw him. As I got closer to him my joy rapidly turned to fear. It was the look on his face that frightened me. I'd never seen him look at me in that way before. I froze. Something was wrong. I didn't want to know what. 'We need to talk', he said. 'OK' was all I could manage, petrified of what was coming next. 'I don't want to see you any more, Catherine. It's over between us.' He had plunged a dagger deep into my heart. The pain was unbearable. I felt physically sick.

I had to know why, what had I done wrong? He didn't want another committed relationship. He felt we were becoming too serious. I struggled to breathe as the meaning of his words seeped into my brain. I ran to the nearest empty classroom. The tears tumbled down my cheeks like Niagara Falls as the memory of our romantic anniversary was left in tatters.

The depth of the pain was overwhelming. I stayed away from college – I couldn't face lectures or seeing him. Several days later, I heard that Anthony had started to date someone else. In my mind, my fears of not being good enough for someone as good-looking and charismatic as Anthony had been confirmed. I had to get away.

I went to stay with some friends in the South of England but I was so distraught after the break-up, struggling to eat and sleep, that the distance and change of scene didn't help. I couldn't stop crying. I thought I would never be happy again.

A few weeks later, I began to worry about the course work I was missing. I had worked very hard, holding down two jobs during my gap year so I could support myself through polytechnic and obtain the diploma. No matter how upset I was, I couldn't let my relationship break-up destroy my goal. I had to try and get on with my life. Putting on a brave face, I went to stay with my parents again for a few days in preparation for my return to Essex.

CHAPTER 3
The return of Anthony

I was at my parents' when the phone rang. It was Anthony. I was shocked to hear his voice. Why was he calling me? I thought he had moved on. Shaking with nervousness, I asked him what he wanted. 'When are you coming back to Essex? Can we meet up?' He asked. He sounded different. He sounded as though he cared about me. Oh my God, could he want me back? I wasn't sure my nerves could handle it. Despite the pain I'd gone through, I was still in love with him. But what about the other woman? There was no way I'd allow three of us to be in the relationship. He reassured me it was all over between them. Perhaps I had been good enough for him after all?

Back together

A few days later I returned to my student house in Essex. I couldn't stop thinking about Anthony as I waited for him to come and see me. I felt excited at the possibility we might get back together, but fearful of getting hurt again. He arrived – the wait was over. The atmosphere was a little strained between us at first. After a while, I relaxed a little. He asked me to go back out with him. A part of me wanted to be strong and say 'No' after what I believed he'd done to me. But, as I looked at him, listened to his soft, sexy voice and remembered how great I felt when things were good between us, I melted. As for the pain, I chose to bury it deep within me.

I dealt with my fear of getting hurt by striving to maintain control of myself, of Anthony and the relationship. I attempted to keep our relationship more casual and less intense. When Anthony asked for space, I gave it to him. I had 'girls' nights out', something I rarely did when we were dating the first time around. Another year flew by. I was finding it difficult to maintain the illusion of a casual relationship.

Six months after my graduation, I left Essex and moved to London in search of a new job. I also went because I was afraid Anthony was falling out of love with me again. I had to show him I wasn't dependent on him, that I could survive without seeing him every day. Once I found work and had established a social life in London, my life seemed to improve. Nevertheless, I was becoming very worried about Anthony and me. Despite the length of our relationship Anthony hadn't mentioned to me what he planned to do or what would happen to us when he graduated in a few months' time. When I first met him, he had been open about his plan to move back to the Canary Islands as soon as he graduated. 'Is this still his plan?' I wondered. 'If so, where do I fit into it, if at all?'

Eventually my anxiety got the better of me. I broached the subject with him, fearful as ever. 'I'm moving back to the Canary Islands as soon as possible', he told me. I waited for him to say 'and I want you to come and live with me. I want to spend the rest of my life with you'. He didn't. Instead he said 'it's up to you what you do'. The only thing he insisted on was that we *didn't* live together.

I felt hurt and rejected. I couldn't imagine my life without him. I had already experienced that and I didn't want to go through the pain again. I had an idea. I could become a teacher as there were plenty of teaching jobs abroad. I enrolled on a TEFL (Teaching English as a Foreign Language) course and made plans to follow Anthony out to the Canaries in the summer, whether he wanted me to or not.

A new life in the Canary Islands

After graduation, Anthony left England as soon as he could. He had hoped to move back to the island where his family lived; however, he was only able to find work on one of the other islands. Thankfully, I managed to find a teaching job on the same island and followed him a month later. I didn't have anywhere to live, though. I asked Anthony if I could stay with him until I found my feet. He reluctantly consented. I thought if we could just live together for a few months, he would see how great it was and wouldn't want me to move out.

My dream of a wonderful life abroad with Anthony was a living nightmare in the first few months. Although I had a teaching job, I had no friends of my own and was totally dependent on Anthony for companionship, support and entertainment. I lay in bed many nights when he was out socialising with his friends, sobbing my heart out. When we did go out together, everyone would speak in Spanish. Not being able to speak the language fluently, I felt left out and lonely. I missed my freedom, my friends and my social life.

I hated the imbalance in our relationship. I felt utterly powerless. And yet I believed it was true love. I was convinced my lack of Spanish was the problem. I thought if I could learn the language quickly, maybe Anthony and I would have a chance of survival. I enrolled on an intensive Spanish course and in many ways it helped. I began to create a life for myself. I was soon enjoying the sunshine, the culture and my new-found freedom.

Not feeling good enough again

While some areas of my life were improving, my relationship with Anthony still wasn't how I dreamed it would be. Although it was great going to the beach together at weekends, having long conversations, sunbathing, swimming and generally enjoying ourselves, there was one major drawback. Anthony was very open about the fact that he enjoyed looking at other women on the beach. We were constantly surrounded by local beauties with their sun-kissed hair and bronzed, voluptuous, bikini-clad bodies. I felt unattractive in comparison. It made me feel very insecure, which I hid by trying to make light of the situation and join in with him. I needed his reassurance that he continued to find me attractive. I didn't receive it.

What made it worse was that I noticed Anthony was now approaching me less often to make love. He was still as gorgeous as ever to me and, as I was taking the contraceptive pill, whenever he felt like making love, I was there, ready and willing. One day Anthony arrived home from work saying he had a present for me. I was surprised. Maybe he still loves me after all? Perhaps he's just stressed about work? What could he have brought me? I wondered. I opened the gift. It was a flesh-coloured sex toy – batteries included! My heart sank. Anthony was eager to try it out. Forever wanting to please him and try and keep us together, I obliged. My heart wasn't in it, though. I felt rejected and not good enough.

More confusing signs

Another year or so passed. Anthony had managed to find a job on the island where his family was based and had moved back in with his parents. I thought this would make him happier and thus help our relationship. But we would have to wait another three months until my teaching contract finished before I could move over to the island and be with him.

I asked Anthony where I'd be living when I moved. 'In with my sister', he informed me. I felt deeply disappointed. Something didn't feel right. It was kind of his sister to offer me a roof over my head and it did make logical sense as there was more room for me there. Nevertheless, I had moved to the Canary Islands to be with him. We had been going out for four and a half years. We had lived together. I had expected him to want us to find a flat together. I also continued to hope that we would get married and have children at some point. As always, fearful of scaring Anthony away, I kept my thoughts to myself.

Before my contract ended, I went to visit Anthony on the other island for the weekend, as I often did. This time, Anthony said he had a surprise for me. After the sex-toy incident, his surprises made me nervous. Whatever it was, he looked happy about it. Was I going to like it, I wondered? 'We are going to see a house', he said. 'The rest of the family are meeting us there.' As we drove up to the house, Anthony explained that he was planning on buying it. I didn't know what to say. I was in shock. There had been no discussion between us about buying a property. What did it mean? What about our future together? I was confused and anxious.

We arrived at the property to find the rest of the family there already. I fought back the tears that were welling up inside me. I felt so insignificant and such an outsider. This was clearly his 'baby' and had nothing to do with me. His family asked me what I thought. What was I to say? 'Yeah, great – just how I'd planned to choose my future marital home after moving lock, stock and barrel out here. Oh and by the way, *is* this my future marital home or is this just a place for you, Anthony?' Instead, I muttered some superficial pleasantries about how lovely it was. I didn't have the courage to speak my truth. I didn't want a scene and I could barely keep it all together. I didn't want Anthony to think I was taking it for granted that I would be living there with him either. I wasn't. I was just hoping I was part of his future vision.

I broached the subject with trepidation a few weeks later. Anthony made it clear that it was much too soon for him to talk about us moving in together properly, let alone marriage. As for the place he was buying, it needed a great deal of work done to it and he seemed in no hurry to move in. I comforted myself with this fact and did my utmost to repress the growing feelings of discord within me.

On the move again

Moving to the other island was a mixed blessing. I longed to see Anthony more often, but dreaded having to start all over again. I knew no-one outside Anthony's family. His family did all they could to make me feel welcome, but I missed having my own friends and my independent life. Living with his sister was not ideal either. I felt unsupported. I felt I had no-one to speak to about how unhappy I was in my relationship, particularly about what I perceived as Anthony's reluctance to commit.

Shortly after I moved in, Anthony went to England on business. He phoned one night and his sister answered. After a while he asked to speak to me. Feeling hurt and rejected because he hadn't asked for me straight away, I hesitantly took the phone. I didn't tell him how I was feeling. I desperately hoped to hear him say how much he was missing me. Instead, he told me he'd been in contact with his ex-girlfriend Lisa. She'd invited him to a party. He was thinking of going. I felt him plunge the dagger deep into my heart yet again. I fought to breathe as the panic started to rise in me. I was petrified he would jump into bed with her. They had such a history and he no longer appeared as interested in me sexually. It was my worst nightmare.

I begged him not to go. I admitted it would devastate me. I was desperate. He said he hadn't made up his mind. I could no longer speak, overwhelmed by my emotions, and hung up. We had a huge row about it when he returned. He assured me he did not go to the party in the end, but I had stopped trusting him.

A few months later, having established a close and supportive friendship with Laura, an American expat, I attempted to re-balance the power and control in my relationship. I decided to stop taking the contraceptive pill. I felt it had enabled Anthony to dictate our sex life. I was also experiencing severe headaches which I thought might be caused by taking the pill for so many years. I chose not to consult him. I felt it was my body and therefore my concern.

Anthony hated using condoms so I knew he would be furious about having to start wearing them after nearly five condom-free years together. He reacted as I predicted. 'At least I feel less vulnerable and more in control now', I told myself, hoping that would make me happy. It didn't.

By now, I was also unhappy in my work. Since moving to the other island, I had supplemented the income from my private English classes with office and receptionist work. None of the work I'd been doing had been remotely related to my polytechnic diploma and I yearned to use the marketing and tourism skills I'd learnt. Chatting to my friend Laura one day about my dilemma, she mentioned that she had a friend who worked for the island's Tourism Department. Soon after our conversation, her friend told me that there was a vacancy, working on a combined public and private tourism initiative. She suggested I apply for the role.

The job sounded really interesting. It meant I'd have the opportunity to travel around the island, visit the top hotels, eat in the best restaurants, deal with marketing and press enquiries and maybe travel overseas too. After a lengthy interview process (including psychometric tests in Spanish!), I was told I had got the job. I was so excited and happy. I felt that it was the beginning of a new adventure for me. I was eager to share my good news with Anthony.

His reaction surprised me. He was not at all happy about it. He said he feared other men would attempt to sleep with me when I was away on business. A part of me was secretly pleased to hear his fears. 'He's afraid of losing me. He must still love me', I thought to myself. Nonetheless, another part of me was angry that he didn't trust me. He also added that he was hoping I would work for him and his family at the English school they were considering opening. I was mystified. I felt he was trying to stifle me and mould me into his ideal woman. I felt totally misunderstood.

Despite my increasing unhappiness in the relationship, I still felt unable to walk away. Anthony was such a big part of my life and I knew, regardless of all our issues, that he was a good person. I also felt a part of his family too. What would they think of me if I ended the relationship? I couldn't bear for them to think badly of me.

The final break-up

I had been doing my tourism marketing job for three months. Anthony and I arranged to meet after work as usual. He told me to wait for him at his parents' flat. He promised to be there at a certain time. His parents were out so I waited alone. What seemed like hours passed. I was getting worried. I hoped nothing had happened to him. I had no idea where he was and no way of contacting him. The later it got, the more I knew that if he'd been in an accident, I would have heard about it. It's a small island and news travels fast. Someone would have called the flat.

The longer I waited, the more my worry turned to anger. When he eventually turned up, I was fuming. I exploded like a volcano. All the anger, unexpressed resentment and hurt that I had been repressing over the years erupted. 'It's over!' I screamed. Anthony laughed. He had never seen me react in such a way. He didn't think I meant it. I had been so dependent on him for so long and had rarely expressed my true feelings during our five-year relationship that I was not surprised. I wanted to leave the flat. I asked him to drive me to his sister's house. I told him again that it was over when he dropped me off. It wasn't easy, nor was telling his sister. I couldn't face his parents. I left that to Anthony. I moved into Laura's flat as soon as I could and buried my feelings of guilt with the assistance of alcohol and work.

CHAPTER 4

Tim – my boss
Brief secondment to the UK

It was incredibly difficult no longer being part of a couple. I felt a huge void in my life. When Anthony tried to persuade me to go back out with him, a part of me wanted to give in and agree to it. Deep down, though, I knew it would only lead to unhappiness. I would not go back for another drug-like fix of him. I had to detox myself. As luck would have it, my boss needed me to go to England to run the office while our UK representative was away.

Being back in England in a different office and speaking in English most of the time helped me to withdraw from my relationship. It was like a form of rehab. As the days passed, I was enjoying the experience so much I didn't really want to go back to the Canary Islands. The problem was I didn't want to give up my job.

Towards the end of my secondment, my Director announced that she was flying over to find a new representation company in the UK for the island. She asked me to accompany her to the bid meetings. We arrived at the first appointment and were escorted to the boardroom where their team were waiting for us. As I sat down, I noticed a good-looking guy with an amazing smile and lovely dimples. He introduced himself as Tim. As the meeting got under way, Tim did most of the talking. 'Not only is he very good-looking, but he seems such a nice, mature, friendly guy. He couldn't possibly be single', I thought to myself. He wasn't wearing a wedding ring, though – not that that meant he was available. All too soon the meeting ended and we said goodbye. I didn't know if I would ever see Tim again, but I hoped I would.

Planning my move

My secondment was over and I returned to the Canary Islands. All the memories came flooding back to haunt me. Then, out of the blue, Anthony's Mum called me. We met for a drink. It was a very uncomfortable experience. I still felt guilty for ending the relationship. I knew the family had become attached to me, as I had to them. I explained my side of the story; I wanted to make her understand why I had ended it. I hoped it would help her to forgive me. Although I still felt guilty and uncomfortable about the situation, at least I now knew that his family didn't hate me as I had feared they would.

A few weeks later I received a welcome distraction. The company Tim worked for had been asked to make a formal bid to our Board. Tim and a colleague arrived to make the presentation. My heart somersaulted when I saw him again. We spent quite some time together during his stay and I found him to be great company. We got on well together. I was really pleased when I discovered he was single; however, I couldn't tell if he was attracted to me at all. He was being very professional.

During Tim's visit, I had the opportunity to find out about the possibility of working back in the UK. If their bid was successful, the company Tim worked for would need a Marketing Assistant, the position I had been in for the last three months. Not only that, but the person would have to work very closely with Tim and would, in the future, have the chance of promotion. The opportunity to return to England, continue to work in the same area, with prospects of promotion, and work closely with Tim . . . Oh, how I wanted that job!

I felt incredibly tense as I waited for the Board to announce which company had won the contract. Finally, the news I'd been hoping for came – Tim's company had been successful. I felt so excited. This was my chance to create a new life for myself back in the UK, but I still had to go through the formal job application procedure. Eventually, Tim called me: I had got the job. I was so happy. I could start again. As I would be making regular business trips to the island, I would still see my Spanish friends and colleagues. I considered myself very lucky.

Living back in England

Although I was eager to move back to the UK and begin my new life, I found the change difficult. Re-adjusting to the British way of life, my new surroundings and my new work colleagues was so hard. With one foot in the Canaries and another in England, I didn't feel as though I belonged anywhere.

I moved back in with my parents, but found it a total shock after seven years of independent living. It was only a few weeks before we admitted the situation wasn't working and I moved in with a friend from polytechnic. Even though three months had passed since Anthony and I had broken up, I felt a big, gaping hole inside of me. To distract myself from the uncomfortable thoughts and emotions I threw myself heart and soul into my work.

Working very closely with Tim helped to ease the pain slightly. The better I got to know him, the more attracted to him I became. He had such a great sense of humour and was always making me laugh, even when we had a heavy workload and looming deadlines. The only problem was that, like Ben, he seemed so friendly with everyone that I couldn't tell how he really felt about me. My self-confidence was low. And after being in a relationship for such a long time, I wasn't sure I could attract another guy.

Getting up close and personal

Tim and I were spending long hours together in the run-up to a major client event. Finally, the night we had been working so hard for arrived. I was too nervous and too busy to eat anything and turned to alcohol in an effort to calm my nerves. Overall, the evening went relatively smoothly and I was relieved when it was over. I was on such an adrenalin high, though, I didn't want to go home. Someone suggested we go to a private members' club in the centre of London to relax and celebrate. It seemed Tim would be going too. I definitely wanted to be there. I managed to grab a light snack at the club, but I was more interested in enjoying the champagne that was flowing, courtesy of my generous colleague. We left the club in the early hours of the morning. Somehow, although it's a bit of a blur because of the amount of alcohol consumed, I ended up spending the night at Tim's. In our inebriated states, we kissed.

The morning after the night before

I awoke the next morning feeling very much the worse for wear. I was unsure whether I could make it through the meeting scheduled for that morning. I knew I would have to go to the office and at least try. Tim and I were also concerned about how we could keep what had happened from the rest of the observant and inquisitive employees. Not that there was really much to say, but we were sure their imaginations would fill in the gaps.

We decided that I would leave Tim's flat first, so that we could arrive separately at the office. I was still wearing the same clothes, which I thought might be a giveaway. As soon as I arrived at the office, though, I had to make a dash to the toilet – several times, in fact, as the effects of the previous night took their toll, which at least took the focus off what I was wearing! I survived the meeting, but vowed never to drink on an empty stomach again.

Over the next few weeks, Tim and I continued to work long hours. As neither of us could be bothered to cook at the end of our working day, we would go to our local restaurant or pub for dinner. This always included alcohol and usually resulted in me spending the night at Tim's. We became great friends. I loved being with him. I loved how he made me feel about myself. He made me feel intelligent and I felt that he believed in me. I felt really supported by him too. Was *this* true love instead, I wondered?

But if this was true love, why hadn't we made love yet? We always laughed so much together, even in bed. Maybe we got on too well as friends? I was getting used to being part of a couple again and liked it a lot, even if we were only 'seeing' each other rather than officially dating as he never actually asked me out. I did find our lack of romance confusing, but I was so happy being with Tim that I pushed it to the back of my mind.

A blow to my heart

One Saturday night several months into our casual relationship, Tim and I were cuddled up in front of the fire watching a romantic comedy when, half-way through the film, he announced he needed to talk to me. It sounded serious. I felt afraid. I turned to face him and braced myself. 'I don't want us to "see" each other any more.' Suddenly, I was right back in the moment when Anthony had dumped me all those years ago. I felt the pain of the dagger piercing my heart once more. The tears rolled down my cheeks. It was so unexpected. What was it about me? Why did I never see this coming? I felt rejected and powerless.

Tim told me it wasn't the right time in his life for a relationship. He had too much going on workwise. He said he was deeply sorry to have upset me. I knew he didn't mean to hurt me. He wasn't that sort of guy. His reasons also made sense. I understood intellectually, but it didn't stop the pain I was feeling. I felt scared. I was alone again, free to fall for another man who might reject me. This time, though, not only had I lost my best friend, but as he was my boss, I would have to face him and work closely with him every day. There was no escape if I wanted to continue doing the job that I loved.

The atmosphere in the office between Tim and me was tense as I adjusted to our less intimate relationship. In addition, I had to endure watching him flirt with other women he came into contact with. However, he did focus his attention on his job, appearing to be virtually married to it. And I made sure we were back to being good friends, carrying on as normal as soon as I could by masking my true feelings and putting on my 'happy face' at work each day.

Over the next five years

During the five years that followed the break-up, some of which is included in the following chapters, Tim and I remained very good friends. We appeared to get on so well and always had so much to talk about. I continued to rely on him emotionally, turning to him for advice and support. I still found him attractive and we even had the occasional drunken kiss. It seemed like true love to me. I was mystified. I thought with the sort of friendship we had, if he didn't want to date me then there must be something wrong with me.

I emotionally tortured myself during those years as we danced around each other. He became another drug-like obsession. Tim had broken up with me because it wasn't the right time in his life. But maybe he was The One? Maybe one day when he had established his career it *would* be the right time and he *would* want to marry me?

CHAPTER 5
Still looking for love in the wrong place

Once more I felt unlovable and lonely. I needed to feel that I was attractive to men. I craved male affection. What if I never had another relationship? What if I never found The One? I couldn't bear the thought. It was too painful. I was desperate to erase the painful feelings and contemplated psychotherapy. A person I knew in the Canaries had benefited greatly from it: maybe it could help me too? A part of me was very tempted. However, another part of me was fearful. I was afraid of the unknown, of facing my pain. I was also afraid of what my colleagues would think about me if they discovered I was seeing a therapist. I cared about what they thought.

I allowed my fears to win and instead of therapy I chose the more common methods of repression and denial. I worked even longer hours and partied harder. I drank excessive amounts of alcohol, ate rubbish and threw myself at almost any man who paid me attention. I had numerous encounters, some of which were more memorable than others.

Ian

I decided to stay with Laura in the Canary Islands for a week. Where better to go, I thought, for some sun, sea and hopefully some sex too! I knew Laura wouldn't judge me as she was very liberal-minded. Shortly after I arrived, Laura arranged for a group of us to go out; among these was Ian, whom she had known for many years. Looks-wise, Ian wasn't my usual type, with his shaved head and head scarf. Nevertheless, he was cute and very charismatic. We flirted with each other all night. At the end of the evening, Ian asked me back to his place. I agreed. I knew I could trust him.

That night I had a realisation. In six years, I had only ever made love to one person, Anthony, who I felt lost interest in me sexually during our relationship. I had to move on, but insecurity overwhelmed me. Would I be able to make love to someone else? I felt like a virgin again. I needed some alcohol to calm my nerves (but not too much as I wanted to stay awake!).

Ian was very understanding and considerate. I knew he had a lot of experience with women from what Laura had told me. As I discovered, he certainly knew what he was doing. I was relieved to find the experience incredibly liberating. After another night of passion, I felt as though I had exorcised Anthony from my body and finally broken the spell he had had on me. It also boosted my self-confidence after what 'didn't' happen with Tim. Ian and I both decided we didn't want to take it any further. It had been perfect as it was: safe, casual, uncomplicated sex.

Glen

Some time later, I made another visit to the Canary Islands. Although I was there on business, I managed to have the last evening to myself and arranged to meet up with Laura and some other friends. Laura's British friend Glen joined us. I had met Glen when I was living on the island. He was very good-looking and a real charmer too, but he also had a reputation for being a bit of a heartbreaker.

Glen flirted heavily with me that evening. I needed the fix and lapped up his attention. I was desperate to feel wanted by a man. I threw caution to the wind and invited Glen back to my hotel room. We sat on the bed and, in varying degrees of undress, proceeded to drink the contents of my mini-bar. Glen passionately embraced me. It was intoxicating. He wanted to take things further. However, dawn was breaking: I would have to leave for the airport in a few hours to catch my flight back to England. I realised it would have been too much of an emotional wrench leaving Glen so soon after making love. Also, because of his reputation, I was doubtful he would ever want a relationship with me. So after kissing him one last time, I asked him to leave and hot-footed it to the airport to catch my flight home, dreaming of what might have been.

Leo

When I wasn't travelling, I took time to reconnect with a group of friends from polytechnic. Leo was part of the group. He was incredibly cute, kind, honest and trustworthy. He wasn't the type to do one-night stands. I began to fall for him. If only we had a chance to spend some quality time together, maybe he could like me back?

One weekend, Leo invited us all to a festival he was working at in his home town. He invited the group to stay at his friend's place for the whole weekend. My work commitments meant I could stay for only one night, but at least I'd get to spend some quality time with Leo. I hoped it was my chance to find love and happiness. Of the group, only myself and another female friend, who was also attracted to Leo (although he'd told the rest of us – but not her – that he didn't feel the same), were single. The other two women in the group were bringing their boyfriends along for the weekend. I felt so left out. I ached to be in a relationship again.

We spent the day at the festival. Leo and I really hit it off, more so than we ever had at polytechnic. We flirted with each other during his breaks and in the bar in the evening when he'd finished work. Afterwards, we went back to the house where we were staying. We were all supposed to sleep in the lounge together (in separate sleeping bags!).

By now, though, my single female friend was extremely upset at seeing Leo and I becoming close. I was too frightened of being verbally attacked by her to go anywhere near her. Instead, I asked Leo if I could sleep somewhere else. He suggested we both sleep in the bedroom. Moments later, sitting on the bed, Leo leant over and kissed me. I was so attracted to him, desperate to be loved and in a relationship, that I ignored my friend's feelings, followed my heart and kissed him back. We spent the night together, kissing, cuddling and talking. I was swept up by the romance of it all. I had to leave early for work the next morning: Leo kissed me goodbye and said he would be in touch. He was a friend. I trusted him. I believed it was the beginning of something special.

As it turned out, things were never the same after that night, either with the group or with Leo. He soon reverted to being a platonic friend. After a while, he stopped contacting me altogether. I was hurt and confused by our brief romantic moment, especially as he had been a friend. 'Maybe I'd have better luck at finding true love with a stranger instead?' I wondered.

David

Another weekend and another opportunity to find love presented itself. I was in the local pub with my flatmates one

Friday night when I was approached by a tall, well-built South African guy, who introduced himself as David. He wasn't like my usual type of guy, but he was very friendly and at least he seemed interested in me. At the end of the evening, David asked me out on a date before we'd even kissed. My self-esteem needed the boost. Finally, I was properly dating again.

At first, we got on quite well. Although I didn't feel particularly physically attracted to him, I thought he might grow on me. Nevertheless, after a few weeks of dating, I realised we had hardly anything in common and our conversations began to dry up. When he invited me back to his bedroom and tried to seduce me, even with my craving for physical intimacy, I needed to feel a spark between us. There was none. I made my excuses and left. One night, fed up with my continually spurning his advances, David ended our brief relationship. Initially, I felt the pain of rejection once more. However, I was relieved not to have to fend him off any longer or to try and convince myself we had a future together. Still unaware of my real needs and self-sabotaging patterns, I blindly and desperately searched on.

Dan

I met Dan when I was working away at an event. He was attractive, suave and sophisticated. He made me laugh and paid me lots of attention. I was flattered and it helped to fill the void within me. Anthony had once said that there were many opportunities to have affairs when away from home on business, in anonymous hotels with colleagues who turned a blind eye . . . I now knew what he meant. It was tempting, especially for someone so unhappily single as me, trying to exorcise and forget the past. It was a chocolate fountain for chocoholics! So, when Dan invited me back to his hotel room after a night of drinking, dancing and flirting, I readily accepted.

The alcohol took its toll and it wasn't long before we fell asleep. It was nice falling asleep in someone's arms. It was something I missed about being in a couple. However, I was awoken shortly afterwards by Dan's loud snoring – an unwelcome cold dose of reality!

As I crept back to my hotel room to sleep the few remaining hours before catching the flight back, I briefly revelled in the boost to my self-esteem caused by my having managed to attract a proper, mature man like Dan. But, it was quickly replaced by guilt and shame, as I remembered that Dan was married and it was clear that I had just been a bit of fun. I tried to convince myself that it was fun too, but once I'd sobered up, it left me feeling empty and alone.

Martin

Despite my experience with Dan, it wasn't long before I embraced another opportunity for a quick fix of male attention and affection. Martin was one of our company's many clients, which added to the element of 'danger' I sensed around him. He was very good-looking, charming and charismatic. He was unmarried too, thankfully.

One night after work during a business trip, Martin and I continued to chat, drink and flirt with each other until the early hours. The sexual tension between us was palpable. The question was, as some of our party were still with us, how would we get together unnoticed? I made my excuses and retired to my hotel room. I waited for a knock at the door: none came, so I changed into my pyjamas and got into bed. Perhaps the attraction I felt between us had all been in my imagination after all. Disappointed in myself, I fell asleep. A short while later I was woken up by the phone ringing next to me. It was Martin. He was in a room a few floors above and wanted to see me. Immediately! My heart was pounding. He was a client. It felt so risqué. I was about to cross a line. I couldn't believe that this was my life, that it was happening to me.

Without changing clothes, I made my way up to Martin's room. The lift door opened and standing there was the night guard! I didn't care. Something magical was about to happen for me. Martin opened the door to his room and embraced me with a passionate kiss. He took me by the hand, led me to his bed and undressed me. I wanted to pinch myself to make sure I wasn't dreaming. It was all so amazing. Then, suddenly, he asked me to turn on to my front. He said he was going to the bathroom to get something which would give me pleasure. The passion drained out of me as fear replaced it. What could it be? Wasn't I enough, especially as it was our first time together?

Returning from the bathroom, he proceeded to caress my skin with a long, cold, metallic object. As he stroked my skin with the object, moving down towards my intimate areas, I realised that if that's what excited him sexually, then he was obviously into stuff that I wasn't. It was time for me to get out of there, fast!

I made my excuses and left as quickly as I could. I giggled uncontrollably as I returned to my room, through the fear and the bizarreness of the experience. When I awoke the following morning, I was dreading having to face him again. But he was a client so it was unavoidable. Wearing our masks of superficiality, which hid so many secrets, we managed to carry on normally with our professional relationship and never spoke of it again.

Tom

I arrived in Dublin for a business event and was excited to read in the paper that an American ship would be docked in the port for a few days. There were around 4,000 American sailors on the loose in the city. Lots of lovely men in uniforms and a chance for an intimacy fix. After work I headed into town with a colleague. The city was heaving with young, fit, male bodies. We managed to get into a bar with a nightclub downstairs. As my colleague and I stood drinking and chatting, a young, handsome, uniformed sailor, complete with sailor's hat, appeared. Thoughts of Richard Gere in the film *An Officer and a Gentleman* floated through my mind as he made his way over to us. We went downstairs to the club and Tom the sailor asked me to dance. My colleague decided to leave us to it and headed back to the hotel. I had a few more drinks, and at some point in my drunken state twisted my ankle dancing. It was quite painful, but luckily the alcohol numbed the pain.

Tom helped me back to his hotel room. He opened the door, threw his sailor's hat on to the chair, scooped me up in his arms and carried me over to his bed. As we lay there kissing and getting more intimate, for a fleeting moment the fact that I was about to give my body to someone I wasn't in a relationship with, a complete stranger this time, drifted across my mind. I buried the thought quickly. I wanted to be left alone to enjoy my fantasy of being swept off my feet by my very own 'officer and gentleman', even if it was just for one night. As it turned out, he was no Richard Gere, but the fact that I could hardly move due to my twisted ankle didn't help.

As soon as the sun came up, I left. I limped back to my hotel, laughing as I thought about the whole experience. It was another fantasy shattered. I knew I would not hear from

Tom again but at least I had a good story to tell my colleagues back in the office the following Monday. I enjoyed making them laugh. Inside, though, the feelings of emptiness returned and I liked myself less because I'd had a one-night stand with a total stranger.

The bath guy

I tried looking for love and happiness closer to home and regularly went clubbing with a friend from work. One clubbing night I got together with a tall, dark and handsome guy. At closing time, the guy invited me back to his place for the night. Under the influence of a lot of alcohol and unable to locate my friend, I accepted. After giving me a brief tour of his flat, he escorted me to his bedroom. By now I was starting to sober up slightly and was a little afraid of what I might have got myself into. I wanted to go to bed to sleep. Determined not to have another one-night stand, I told him I was too drunk to do anything. He was also very drunk. Thankfully, though, he was a trustworthy guy and was happy just to go to sleep beside me.

The next morning he got up really early and I heard him running a bath. I pretended to be asleep. I was so embarrassed. As I lay there, I heard loud splashing noises coming from the bathroom as he appeared to be having the noisiest bath ever. 'What on earth could he be doing in there to make that much noise?' I wondered, innocently. It was obviously something he wanted to do in private, which freaked me out as I'd only just met the guy. He returned from the bathroom looking rather self-conscious. I decided it was time for me to leave and made a swift exit.

The one I threw up on

A few weeks later I met another guy at the club. Once more, I had had far too much to drink and, finding him very cute and my friend long gone, I accepted his offer to go back to his place. In order to get to his bedroom we had to walk past the lounge where his flatmates were sitting around. He seemed pleased that they had seen us. However, we hadn't been sitting on his bed for long when I started to feel queasy. Before I could do anything about it, I threw up all over him and on a part of the bed, instantly destroying any possibility of romance in the process! I wasn't embarrassed until I woke up in the morning and the memory of what happened came flooding back. All I could do was apologise and leave as quickly as possible. As I passed the lounge on my way out, his flatmates all laughed at me. I was mortified. It didn't stop me from sharing the story with my work colleagues on Monday, though. My reputation as a 'good-time girl' was growing. I liked being seen as a fun, liberated woman. I also wanted my colleagues, especially Tim, to know that guys were attracted to me. My self-esteem needed it.

The radio DJ

Another night at the club I met a gorgeous guy with a distinctive, sexy voice. He told me his name and that he was a radio DJ for a reasonably well-known radio station. I thought he was joking, but at least it was a different chat-up line from the ones I was used to. He seemed a really nice guy and we hit it off. It wasn't long before we were kissing. However, at some point, he told me he had a girlfriend. I guessed it was true. Why would a good-looking and charming guy like him be single? I went home feeling very dejected.

The following afternoon I decided to listen to the radio station he said he worked for. I heard his distinctive sexy voice once again. He hadn't been joking. His programme was a request show. I nervously picked up the phone and dialled the number for the radio station. The call went directly to him, and the next thing I knew, I was speaking to him again. We had a quick chat off-air while a record was playing. It was surreal. I wanted him to know the emotional pain I felt he'd caused me by leading me on and then telling me he had a girlfriend. So I asked him to play 'Love is a Battlefield' by Pat Benatar and we brought the call to an end. I listened for the rest of the afternoon, hoping to hear my song. He didn't play it for me. I felt miserable and tried to console myself with the fact that, if nothing else, I had another story to entertain my friends and colleagues with on Monday.

Although I was enjoying my popularity and reputation at work due to my night-time exploits, inside I was finding it hard to deal with the brief encounters. I was tiring of the continual highs of attracting someone new, followed by the incredible lows of rejection and disappointment when it went wrong. I was tired of all the strangers, but remained desperate for someone to hold me and love me.

Nigel

Nigel was far from a stranger to me as we worked for the same company. That was a part of his appeal. Nigel was open, friendly, funny and smooth-talking. He was very attentive, a great listener and he made me laugh. At the end of one particular working day, following a run of several disappointing, unsuccessful romantic encounters, I needed to pour my heart out to someone. It had to be a man. I needed another fix of male attention in order to feel that, despite my seemingly endless single status, I was still attractive and worth dating.

Nigel was there for me. His fiancée happened to be away at the time. He took me to a local Italian restaurant and wined and dined me. When he invited me back to his place, I accepted. It was wonderful to be with someone who I felt was a supportive, if somewhat flirtatious, friend instead of a total stranger. That night, his charm, smooth talking and several bottles of wine seduced me. 'Would he leave his fiancée for me?' I lay there wondering that night. In the cold light of day, though, despite being flattered at the thought, I wasn't sure it was something I actually wanted.

Two more intimate encounters with Nigel later, I realised I would never have the special relationship that I desperately wanted if I continued to see him. I wanted to be the one getting married, although I hoped my guy would be faithful to me. I felt ashamed at how low I felt I had sunk in my quest to find true love. I made a decision not to be physically intimate with Nigel again and distanced myself from him as much as I could while working with him.

Richard

Shortly after I made this decision the politics and stress at work became overwhelming. I was an emotional wreck. I needed yet another fix of male attention and support to ease the pain. I turned to Richard, a business contact. He had always been very friendly towards me. When I called Richard, he offered to take me to dinner that night.

Soon after arriving at the restaurant, he poured me a much-needed glass of wine, which I swiftly drank. Several more glasses and a light meal later, a part of me was feeling much better. I was enjoying Richard's attention. My problems and reality faded into the background. As the night progressed, the alcohol continued to flow. At some point in the evening, we kissed. It was a line I crossed which I later deeply regretted. He thought I wanted an affair. I did not.

I did not have the courage or strength to be honest about my feelings towards him and instead did my best to give him the brush-off while trying to maintain a friendly, but professional, relationship. I felt as though I was constantly walking on eggshells. Rather than solve my problems, I had created more pain and stress for myself.

On some level I realised that enough heartache was enough. I needed a fresh start. And so I made a commitment to myself: I would be totally celibate for a period of six months. I was going to wait until I was asked out on a proper date, by someone who was uninvolved with anyone else. There would be no physical or emotional intimacy whatsoever until there had been some genuine romance. Maybe that would lead me to The One?

CHAPTER 6

John ~ the vegetarian
Could I have spotted The One?

A round the beginning of my celibate period, I went to an event overseas. Part of my role during the week included attending a press interview with a journalist. I was very nervous about meeting the journalist as he had a reputation in our office for being a little difficult. I was warned to be properly prepared.

It was time for the meeting. I made my way to the meeting room and knocked on the door. John opened it. He wasn't at all what I had expected. There was something about him that I really liked. He was a complete contrast to the smooth-talking charmers I was used to. In addition, I sensed he had a warm heart beneath his cool, aloof and professional manner. He was attractive, too. I was smitten.

After the interview I longed to speak to John again, but I had no professional reason to do so. I watched him from a distance, though. He looked so serious. My heart went out to him: I wanted to rescue him, to give him my love and make him happy. However, John wasn't the sort of guy that I should either chase personally or upset professionally. And I'd made a commitment to myself to be celibate. I would just have to satisfy myself with daydreaming about him instead.

The experience of celibacy

Daydreaming about getting together with John sometime in the future was safe. It helped me to survive the months of celibacy, particularly in the moments when I wasn't completely absorbed by my work. I mentally willed John to want me as I wanted him. The fantasising, coupled with the long hours at work, made time pass quickly. Before I knew it, my period of celibacy was nearly over.

It was time for another business trip abroad. I was taking a group of representatives with me on the trip, and the publication John worked for would be sending someone. I was willing it to be him. A few days before we were due to fly out, I received the news: John would be joining us on the trip. I couldn't believe my luck. As I waited for the group to arrive on the day we were departing, I felt very nervous about seeing him again, especially as I knew we'd be spending most of the week together. I hoped it wouldn't be obvious how I felt about him. It wouldn't look very professional.

During the trip, I did my utmost to appear business-like and emotionally detached, reminding myself how carefully I had to tread because of our working relationship. John appeared equally business-like and unemotional. I could not detect any personal interest in me whatsoever on his part. An aspect of me preferred the safety of daydreaming, since at least in my fantasy world he was attracted to me. I was dreading the reality of rejection, but I wanted to know how he felt about me.

On the last night of the trip, we went to a local bar to unwind. Afterwards, John invited us all back to his hotel suite. I had had a few drinks, but not too many as I wanted to maintain control of myself and not do something I would regret later. This was my last chance to find out whether or not John was attracted to me. Seeing him out on his balcony alone, I took the opportunity to go and speak to him. We made idle conversation for a while, yet I still could not detect even a glimmer of attraction. I had obviously lost my touch. Some of the group then came to join us and my chance was over. I returned to England the next day feeling very down.

Back in the office, my mood sank even lower as the post-trip blues set in and the reality of my empty love life hit me once more. I consoled myself with the thought that I had made it through the six-month period of celibacy, so at least my self-respect had been slightly restored.

A new relationship

A few days later, I received a call at the office. It was John. My body started to shake with nervousness as I heard his voice. 'What could he be calling me for?' I wondered. He asked me for a transparency, an image to accompany the article he was writing following our trip. 'Of course, silly me', I scolded myself internally. My job was to provide such things. That was what I was there for! At the end of our brief conversation, I was about to put the phone down when, right out of the blue, John asked me if I would go out for a drink with him. I nearly fell off my chair. It was such a surprise! He made my day. I wanted to share my joy with the whole office, but I refrained. I was concerned about my position professionally, especially with my track record of relationships.

Being asked out on a proper date again was a boost to my self-esteem, especially as it was with someone I'd liked for several months rather than a total stranger. It seemed as though my decision to wait until I was asked out on a date before becoming intimate on any level with a guy had paid off. I felt pleased with myself.

The night of the date arrived. I was feeling extremely anxious. Not only was I going on a date with an industry journalist, but it was also my first proper date in quite a while. I felt out of practice, particularly regarding dating etiquette. I had got it wrong so many times since splitting up with Anthony. I didn't want to jeopardise my chance with John by sleeping with him too soon. I was afraid that if I slept with him too soon he might think I wasn't good enough to date, but that if I waited too long, he might think I was frigid and lose interest. These were things I hadn't concerned myself with before. It seemed like a minefield.

We arranged to meet at a pub in central London straight after work, so at least I didn't have to worry about what to wear. I had a drink to calm my nerves. I drank it slowly to maintain control over my behaviour. During the evening, I discovered that John was a fascinating guy and much more personable outside work. He seemed extremely intelligent, very sweet, kind and caring. He was a great listener and attentive too. He also had a dry sense of humour. I found myself very attracted to him.

At the end of the date John walked me to the train station. I had fantasised about being with him for ages and I longed to be in a relationship. I really hoped he was going to kiss me and ask me out again. As I said goodbye, he leant over and kissed me and I got my wish.

I realised then that I would be making my way home across London on my own. The part of me that believed in true love was hoping John would accompany me back to my flat, to make sure I got home safely. I kept my thoughts to myself, though. As he rightly said, we lived on opposite sides of the city and it would have meant him spending ages travelling back across London. That wouldn't have made sense. Inside, though, I felt disappointed. Nevertheless, I ignored my heart and went with the logic. At least I had another date with a guy I really liked.

On the next date we went to dinner. That night, I discovered John was a vegetarian. He was so serious about it that he informed me he wouldn't kiss me if I'd been eating meat. My heart sank as I heard the words. Once again I felt disappointed and a little rejected. This hadn't formed part of my romantic plan. Nonetheless, a part of me admired the fact that he felt so strongly about something and that he was sticking to his values. I wanted to keep him happy and so I ignored my own needs and preferences and decided to be a vegetarian too. He was worth it.

We were getting on well and I was enjoying John's company. So, several dates later, when it seemed that it was more than a fling, I felt ready to take our relationship to the next level and invited John to stay over at my place. The experience was akin to the first kiss. There was definitely a real attraction between us, but the intense chemistry I felt in the early stages with Anthony was not there. However, being with Anthony had resulted in heartache for me and I knew that, even with the chemistry, Anthony hadn't been The One. Maybe *this* was true love after all? Maybe John was The One? I was hopeful.

Despite the fact that John was unmarried and living alone, he asked me not to tell anyone, apart from my family and flatmates, that we were dating. He said he did not want attention drawn to his personal life at work. Initially, I thought it would be convenient for me too. Deep down, though, it didn't feel right. Desperate to keep my partner happy and maintain the relationship, I ignored my feelings and wore my mask of pretence, hiding the truth from colleagues and friends in the business.

Confusion reigns

The longer I spent with John, the more complicated, challenging and uncomfortable it became to maintain the illusion. Even five months after we started going out, I still had to pretend that John and I weren't dating when we happened to attend the same conference. I was there with my boss and several clients, all of whom knew John professionally and were staying at the same hotel.

I was mortified to discover that my boss was staying in the room just along the corridor from me. I was on tenterhooks every morning as I crept back to my room, hoping not to be seen so that I could make my boss think I had spent the night alone!

Apart from getting together at night, John would only speak to me in public if no-one we knew was around. Although a part of me found it exciting to have this element of danger in our relationship, another part of me hated the secrecy. I felt that if he truly loved me he would be proud to be with me and wouldn't care what others thought about us. I was happy to act professionally, but it felt wrong to lie. 'If we were married, it would be very different', I thought to myself.

It wasn't only when we were working together that John maintained his distance. There were generally no 'PDA's' (public displays of affection). Unlike me, he didn't like holding hands or kissing when we were out in public. I longed for more physical affection. As time went by I became increasingly disillusioned. We didn't seem to laugh together or have any spontaneous, childlike fun either. After a while, I felt more alone and unloved when I was with him than when I was physically on my own. Consequently, the longer we dated, the worse I felt about myself.

Having to keep our relationship a secret and the lack of intimacy (outside of the bedroom) were two aspects. Another was that I had put John on a pedestal intellectually. There was no doubting his intelligence, but often when I was with him, I felt stupid. The situation was worse when we went out with his friends, many of whom, like John, had had a university education. My self-esteem was gradually being eroded. I felt unlovable and not good enough again.

The inevitable break-up

After one year of dating, I realised that I was very unhappy in the relationship. I wanted to find true love more than I wanted just to be with someone. I had to end it. Despite my emotional pain, I found it hard to tell John it was over between us. I hadn't stopped liking him, but he wasn't The One.

John seemed surprised when I ended it. He couldn't see what was wrong. I knew what that was like – I had been there. However, I didn't do it to hurt him. I did it to stop me from hurting any more. I was alone again, and even more confused about what true love looked like. But at least now I had a good idea of what it *didn't* look like.

CHAPTER 7

Harry – the guy with the Porsche

A traffic light party

Unhappily single once more, I realised that in a year's time I would be 30 and I still hadn't found The One. I was scared, in danger of being 'left on the shelf'. My friend invited me to a Traffic Light Party. Even though I had only just broken up with John, ever hopeful of finding true love I decided to go.

My friend had to tell me what a Traffic Light Party actually was as I had no idea. Apparently, people who are in a relationship wear something red to the party; those who are 'not sure' or want to keep their options open wear something yellow or amber; and people who want to advertise the fact that they are single and very much open to offer wear something green. I liked the concept. It would make a refreshing change to know whether or not the person I was attracted to was available without even speaking to them. I chose to wear something amber and something green. I had such a hard time trying to say 'No' to people that this seemed an easier method of fending off any unwanted advances.

We arrived at the party and immediately headed to the bar. I was very happy to see a plethora of guys wearing amber or green, some of whom were very attractive. It could be a good night. Having drunk a glass of wine, I felt brave enough to mingle. It wasn't long before I got chatting to a handsome guy sporting a green top. I was enjoying the light flirting and attention until we began discussing our domestic situations. My new friend, who was in his late twenties, confessed that he still took his dirty laundry round to his mum every week; she still washed and dried his clothes for him, and did his ironing too. He admitted that he doted on her. I knew then that he was definitely not The One for me. I needed rescuing, quickly.

My knight appears

Suddenly, a handsome stranger appeared by my side. Sensing my desire to move, my 'knight' acted as though we already knew each other and steered me safely away to a quiet corner of the pub. I thanked him for rescuing me and assumed that would be it. But, luckily for me, he didn't seem in a hurry to walk away. Harry offered to buy me a drink. We spent the rest of the evening drinking, chatting, flirting and getting to know each other.

As the night wore on, I found that Harry was not only incredibly good-looking, he was also very charming and funny. I was really enjoying his company and I felt so attracted to him. I hoped he felt the same about me. Several drinks later, things were heating up between us. Finally, Harry pulled me close to him and kissed me. I was swooning. He asked for my telephone number. 'Is this the start of something special? Have I found true love at last?' I went home feeling on cloud nine. 'Thank goodness I was brave enough to end my relationship with John', I thought to myself.

Is this The One?

The next morning, I woke up feeling a little the worse for wear. Had last night all been a dream? He said he'd call me, but would he really? In the cold light of day, I had my doubts. However, later that day he called. I was relieved and excited. He asked if he could take me out to dinner the following night. He said he would drive over and pick me up from my flat and drop me home after the date. I couldn't believe my luck. I knew he didn't live that far away, but I wasn't expecting him to go to this much effort so soon. I wasn't used to being treated so well.

I couldn't wait to get home from work and get ready for my date. As I was getting ready, my male flatmate decided to lean out of the open flat window waiting for Harry to appear so he could embarrass me. Soon I heard him shouting at the top of his voice, 'Harry's here. He's driving a Porsche!' My emotions were all over the place as I felt embarrassed by my flatmate, but proud of the fact that my new boyfriend had an impressive car. I finished getting ready as quickly as I could and a few minutes later our dream date was under way.

Harry took me to a lovely, intimate Italian restaurant. During the evening, I discovered that, in addition to being incredibly handsome and having an impressive car, Harry had great taste in clothes and in food and wine. He also had a good job and was much closer to me in age than John was. He made me laugh and was warm and affectionate too. Despite it being our first date, I felt comfortable and relaxed with him. The whole evening was magical. I longed for another date.

Later that week he took me out again. He said he was taking me to a local pub with his flatmate and some other friends. Throughout the evening he was openly affectionate with me, holding my hand, stroking the back of my neck, hugging me and kissing me. He seemed proud to be with me. I felt loved and admired.

A couple of dates later and I felt that my love life could hardly be any better. I really enjoyed Harry's company, all the affection and attention he lavished on me, and the way he made me feel when I was with him. I even introduced him to my family, who told me they thought he was great too. 'Are my unhappy single days finally behind me?' I wondered.

The cracks appear

Over the next few weeks, Harry frequently took me out to dinner. So that we could enjoy a bottle or two of wine together, I would usually stay at his place for the night. That way he didn't have to drive me home. When we went to bed, Harry was happy to kiss and cuddle me and then fall asleep. At first, I found it incredibly romantic and loving. It made me feel safe with him. The closer we got, the more my desire for him increased. But, he didn't appear to feel the same.

The longer we dated, the more I worried. How could he be so attentive, considerate and affectionate with me in every other way and yet not have sex? What was wrong with me? I was sure he wasn't cheating on me. He wasn't the type and he wouldn't have the time.

I was very confused and started to feel insecure again. It reminded me a little of when I was seeing Tim, but at least Harry was open about dating me and he was romantic too. However, I had a deep feeling in the pit of my stomach that something was not right about our relationship. I felt powerless to change the situation but did my best to figure out what the problem was in the hope that I might find a solution.

Harry liked to let his hair down after work and at weekends. Consequently, he would frequently be too wasted to do much except fall asleep. I wondered if that was the reason for him not wanting sex, or if he was using it as an excuse not to make love because he wasn't attracted to me physically. I wanted him to open up to me, to tell me the truth about what was going on, but he wouldn't.

Perhaps it was because his female flatmate was always around? Or maybe he was afraid of getting too close to someone again after his previous girlfriend had hurt him so badly? It wasn't my place to ask his flatmate to give us some space and I certainly couldn't change Harry's painful past.

One night Harry announced that he was taking me away to the coast for the weekend, staying overnight in a hotel. Romantic images of a candlelit dinner followed by a night of passion filled my mind. As we drove to the coast that weekend, my hopes were raised as I realised I would finally be making love with my handsome boyfriend later that evening. Unfortunately, my hopes were all that were raised as Harry proceeded to get very drunk after dinner, rendering himself unfit to do anything that night, or even the next day! Before I knew it, we were on our way back home again. I felt deeply disappointed and utterly bewildered.

Perhaps Harry could still change. I had been studying psychology and counselling at night school for a year and suspected that Harry needed professional help. I gently suggested he might want to contact a counsellor or therapist to assist him to work through the pain of his last relationship and help him move on. He didn't take the suggestion well.

Another break-up

Being with Harry had been so wonderfully different from being with John in the beginning. It had been much closer to what I imagined a loving relationship, perhaps even true love, would feel like. Six months later, though, I felt let down and more confused than ever. I started to think about John again, remembering the good times we'd had and the fact that we had had sex, and often, during our relationship. Had I made a mistake in breaking up with him? What if he had been The One after all? My mind was in turmoil.

Harry and I had arranged to go on holiday together for some sun and sea – and, I hoped, for some sex too. It had been planned for several months. It now looked as though it was going to be a sex-free two weeks! I couldn't face that. Harry was too handsome. It would be too frustrating. I could not and would not endure the façade of our so-called relationship any longer: I told him it was over. He broke down. I was astonished. Despite feeling compassionate towards him and not wanting to see him suffer, I stuck to my decision.

Work had been incredibly stressful too so I decided to go on the holiday by myself! I knew that the change of scene would do me some good, even though the reality of my unhappy single state would be there waiting for me when I got back again. When would the pain stop and true love begin?

CHAPTER 8

The return of John
Unhappily single again

Whenever I found myself single, the familiar void returned. This time was no exception. I ached to be held and have someone be there for me. I needed my drug-like fix of love and affection. I felt time was against me. I was afraid to wait, to take the chance that someone new might show up and want to be with me. What if they never appeared? I couldn't handle that. Instead, I turned my thoughts to John. He had been upset when I had ended our relationship. Would he consider taking me back, I wondered?

The company I was now working for was organising an industry event abroad. I assumed John would be attending the event and, sure enough, when I scanned the list of delegates, there was John's name. I hadn't seen him in almost seven months. In the run-up to the event I felt like a nervous teenager as I anxiously waited to see him again, hoping he would give me a second chance.

The event started. John and I were in the same location at last. Nevertheless, each day I had to satisfy myself with just seeing him in passing as work kept us both very busy. The week passed rapidly and suddenly it was the final event party. This was my last chance to speak to John before we went back to our separate worlds. I watched him for most of the night, waiting for an opportunity to catch him alone. It came. Full of 'Dutch courage', I asked John if I could talk to him in private. He said yes. It was a good sign. We went up to my hotel room.

Being honest

'If only I could combine the positive aspects of Harry and John into one person,' I thought to myself, 'then I'd be with The One.' I did my best to make the impossible happen in the hotel room that night as I told John what I believed had been wrong with our relationship, in order to give him the opportunity to make it work a second time.

When I'd finished talking I looked expectantly at John, hoping to hear him say 'I agree with everything you've said. I do want you back and I promise I will change'. However, the words he uttered took me completely by surprise. 'I'm seeing someone.' Why had I not thought of that? He was a really nice guy. It made sense. Nevertheless, he went on to admit that his relationship was not serious and that he still had feelings for me. He said he needed time to think. I gave him a hug and then he left.

A second chance

Six weeks later, John called. Was I about to be given another chance at finding true love? It appeared so. John told me that he still missed me and wanted to try again, now that he was single. He promised things would be different. I believed him; after all, he knew what I wanted as I had explained it all to him. If he loved me he would change his ways and do what I felt was needed to help us have a loving relationship, wouldn't he?

For the first three months, everything was wonderful. Even though John still wouldn't tell his colleagues we were dating, he seemed much more relaxed, loving and openly affectionate with me, both in public and in private. I also felt he was much more attentive and considerate of my needs. He really had changed. It was also great to have a sexual relationship with someone I loved and felt attracted to again. All it had taken was open communication to have the relationship I wanted. Had I finally found true love?

By now, John was planning to move out of his rented accommodation and was considering buying a property. Would he ask me to move in with him? I hoped he would. 'He's in his late thirties. He has taken me back. He must be thinking about settling down with me soon, surely', I thought to myself.

It soon transpired that my romantic idyll was just a honeymoon phase as John announced that he had found the flat he was looking for and had put in an offer. He wouldn't be asking me to move in with him. He didn't feel ready for that. The familiar feelings of pain and rejection returned. At the same time, it also felt as though John was withdrawing from me both physically and emotionally as the public and private displays of affection were diminishing rapidly. I felt our relationship slipping back to the way it was before we broke up. My unhappiness returned with a vengeance.

Although my heart was aching, my logical mind reminded me that I was going to be 30 soon and if I wasn't going to be living with John, I should buy my own place. As I did not have a deposit for a flat, I would have to move back in with my parents in order to save up the money. In six months' time I should have enough money to buy somewhere. 'Or, maybe John will be so in love with me by then that he'll ask me to move in with him!' I thought, forever the optimist.

Turning 30

It was the weekend before I turned 30. Although my actual birthday was on a Wednesday, John told me he was taking me somewhere special, and expensive, for a celebratory dinner the following Saturday night. It was a very thoughtful and kind gesture on his part. Nevertheless, I longed to celebrate on the Wednesday night as I felt it was such a milestone for me. In an attempt to satisfy my needs, I called a few friends and arranged for us to go out to dinner in central London after work. I invited John too. I really hoped he would say yes. But he refused, saying he'd be bored as we'd be talking 'shop' all night. I struggled to contain my hurt and disappointment.

I woke up feeling very ill on the day of my 30th birthday. I had a bad cold and was feeling very low. I lay in bed, briefly contemplating my life. Nothing had turned out the way I had imagined or hoped it would. I had envisaged myself married to The One by the time I was 25 and having had my first child by now. Here I was, 30 years old, back living with my parents, in a relationship with someone I wasn't even sure was The One, with no sign of us moving in together, let alone a marriage proposal or a baby. I felt incredibly unhappy.

That night, I turned to alcohol in my unconscious attempt to numb the pain. I put on my 'happy face' and tried to have fun. I secretly wished John would do something romantic and totally out of character by turning up at the restaurant to surprise me. But he didn't. One of my friends told me her boyfriend was driving all the way from Surrey into central London to pick her up and drive her home, just because she'd asked him to. It wasn't even her birthday. Why couldn't I have a boyfriend like that? I didn't understand what was wrong with me. I needed more alcohol to deaden the increasing pain.

A few weeks later, I contemplated breaking up with John again but I couldn't bring myself to do it. What if I broke up with him and then realised afterwards that he was The One after all? I wouldn't be able to win him back a third time. I knew that. It would mean my life would be over. Rather than risk making the 'wrong' decision, I chose to stay stuck in turmoil. It seemed easier somehow, despite my unhappiness.

Dark days

'Maybe I need therapy? Perhaps that could help?' I often thought. However, I was still too afraid. I was afraid of the unknown and of confronting my painful past. I was also fearful a therapist might tell me to leave John. Where would I be then? Yes, I was unhappy, but the unhappiness was at least familiar to me and, therefore, more comfortable than the alternative. I continued to do my best to repress and deny my feelings instead, but other areas of my life were being affected too.

The cold I had had on my 30th birthday developed into full-blown flu a week later. Anxious about taking time off and feeling overwhelmed by the amount of work I knew would be piling up in my absence, I forced myself to go back before I was well enough, denying my body the time it needed to recover fully in the process. My health steadily deteriorated as a consequence.

New Year's Eve arrived. It should have been a time of personal celebration for me as I was in a steady relationship with an attractive, intelligent and kind man. In addition, I had a good job with a generous salary. Underneath, though, I had lost heart in both my relationship and my job. I felt incredibly stressed and utterly exhausted. Inside I was slowly cracking up mentally, physically and emotionally.

A ray of light in the darkness

Later that January, I turned to Laura for support. She asked me some very thought-provoking questions during our telephone conversation. My unhappy relationship faded momentarily into the background as I focused on my career. Consequently, I realised that when I was doing the evening class in psychology and counselling I had felt happier than I had in a long time. My life had felt more meaningful.

I knew then that I wanted to work in the helping profession. I also wanted to feel as intelligent as John and his university-educated friends. Laura encouraged me to go for my dream and inspired me to research my options. I discovered that there was a three-year full-time university degree course in psychology and counselling. I applied, even though a part of me was concerned that, at the age of 30, I wouldn't fit in.

'If I am accepted on to the course, I'll need all the money I can save to fund my career change', I realised. I knew it would mean that I'd have to endure my stressful job for another seven months, until August. 'At least I'll feel better about leaving my job then, as it will give my boss enough time to find someone to replace me.' I had it all worked out.

Breaking point

Two months later, my body appeared to have stopped co-operating with me almost completely. I felt constantly ill and had no energy. I had to accept the fact that I did not have the physical or emotional strength to endure the painful feelings of rejection and loneliness in my relationship any more.

Whatever John and I had together, I now knew it wasn't true love. I had to end it once and for all. I could not deal with confrontation at the best of times, least of all now, and so I sent John a letter. I felt a sense of relief afterwards. I didn't realise what a draining effect constantly fretting over whether John was The One had had on me until it was all over.

I still liked John, but he definitely wasn't The One. Why had it taken me two and a half years to realise it? Why did I need these drug-like fixes of male attention and affection? Why couldn't I handle being alone? Why hadn't I found true love and happiness? I was about to embark on a journey of discovery that would answer all of these questions.

CHAPTER 9

Beginning to look for love in the right place

The answers are in M.E.

My health was getting even worse. I was finding the journey into work exhausting. In addition to the incredible exhaustion, all day long I was experiencing painful muscle cramps and sensitivity to light and sound. I would sit at my desk feeling overwhelmed by the amount of emails requiring a response from me and would pray the phone didn't ring. When it did, I broke down in tears. I couldn't cope any more. I had to resign.

I assumed my health problems were stress-related. I believed I just needed a two-week break to regain my strength. After that, I would then do some temp work. That way, I could continue to save the money I needed to do the degree course I had now been accepted on, which was due to start in the autumn.

I had a rest for two weeks. I didn't feel any better after it. Following several visits to the doctor, I was finally diagnosed with M.E. (Chronic Fatigue Syndrome). Overnight, my world fell apart. Although a part of me was relieved to discover exactly what was wrong with me, I was horrified to hear that there was no cure, no magic pill. In addition, the doctor could not tell me how long it would be before I would get better – or even if I would get better at all.

I was very scared. The doctor had said the medical profession could not cure me, nor was there anything to take away the pain. The diagnosis meant that I could not work, never mind be the sociable party girl any more. These were the things I felt defined me. Even some of the people I had believed to be my friends no longer seemed to be interested in me because I couldn't go out. What chance would I have at finding true love now?

I was 30 years old, living with my parents, with so little energy that I couldn't even both have a bath and wash my hair in the same day, let alone go out and meet people or earn a living. The fear, loneliness and confusion, coupled with the inability to relate to anyone, my loss of identity and my chance of going to university having been stripped from me, left me in a very, very dark place. I felt the illness was a curse, something that had the potential to ruin my life – if I let it.

Over the years, under layers of pretence, repression and denial, I'd lost sight of who I was. My self-esteem was at rock bottom. 'The One' I had to focus on in order to heal and give myself any chance of true love and happiness in the future was *me*! With no energy to distract myself with work and no-one for company during the day, I began to examine myself and my life. I perceived the degree course as something that would help me feel more intelligent and fulfilled and therefore make me happier. Hence, I was ready and willing to do anything, including undergoing psychotherapy, if it meant I could be well enough to begin the course in September.

A therapy virgin

At the beginning of therapy my level of self-awareness was relatively limited. I did not know myself in terms of my beliefs, my patterns, my emotions or my behaviours. I un-consciously reacted to people and situations around me automatically, with no idea as to why. I was unaware of the problems I had caused myself by denying and repressing all the emotional pain I had felt over the years through the numerous boyfriends and male encounters. I was a 'yes' person, afraid to say 'no', fearful that it would stop people from liking me or lead to a confrontation. This level of self-awareness had to change if I was to find true love and happiness. The time had come to really know myself (see Secret One in Part Two of this book).

The process was not without its challenges, though. I had to face the fact that I had played the role of a victim most of my adult life, blaming others for my pain and unhappi-ness. I had blamed my parents, my ex-boyfriends, the male encounters and many others. The therapist explained that it didn't mean that everything that ever happened to me was my fault, rather that it was my responsibility to deal with my feelings, especially my anger and resentment, about what had happened to me and for what I'd done over the years.

However, the benefits of therapy far outweighed the challenges. Through the process I started to understand myself properly. The therapist was able to help me to see things about myself and my behaviours that I had been blind to. She helped me to understand why I had made the choices I had, particularly in terms of looking for love and in rela-tionships. I began to see that I had neglected my needs for a long time, and I came to understand why I had treated myself so badly and the effect that had had on my self-esteem. I discovered how I'd disempowered myself by living a life dominated by fear; why I had repeatedly settled for second best, for unhappiness, and why I kept attracting the 'wrong' men for me.

In therapy I discovered that in order to transform the relationship with myself and find true love, I needed to stop these behaviours and commit to being true to myself (see Secret Three). I learnt to teach others how to treat me and how to treat myself better; subsequently, I ceased to be a 'yes' person. This comes naturally to some people but after years of fearful living and mistreating myself, it was a steep but vital learning curve for me. It was a relief to be able to change and begin to create a new life for myself.

Self-Help

In addition to psychotherapy I watched many Oprah Winfrey TV shows and followed the advice of the experts that appeared on them. When I had the energy, I devoured self-help books too, not only reading them but actually carrying out the exercises. My friend Laura had lent me *How to Heal Your Life* by Louise Hay five years previously. At that time, I was not ready to face myself. I skim-read the book without doing the exercises. Now, though, I understood how important it was and I was willing to change.

From all of this I discovered that I didn't love myself and that it was essential to learn to love myself if I was ever to find true love and happiness (see Secret Two). Learning to like myself, never mind love myself, was not only alien to me, it was also incredibly uncomfortable as I felt extremely unlovable. I realised I had many emotional layers to let go of from the past in order to feel what I wanted to feel about myself. Although therapy and self-help were assisting me, it was not a quick or linear process.

Two steps forward and three steps back

One week a friend invited me out for a drink. Because of my fluctuating energy levels, it was touch and go as to whether I could make it. When the day arrived I decided I did have the energy. When we got to the bar, desperate to feel normal again and more like my old self, I agreed to share a bottle of wine with my friend. A mature guy at the next table took an interest in us and we got chatting to him. We were just being friendly as he was in town alone on business. He bought us more wine. In the end my friend and I consumed a whole bottle each.

My friend's new boyfriend then turned up and they left to go to dinner. I stayed talking to the stranger. We talked until the bar closed, at which point he invited me back to his hotel. I was suddenly very frightened. This felt very different from my clubbing days. I didn't want to go back to my parents: it didn't feel right, but I certainly didn't want to go anywhere with the stranger. I wanted to be rescued again, by a man. I turned to my faithful friend Tim, who was still there for me when I needed him, some five years after we broke up. I called him, explained the situation and asked if I could stay at his place. He agreed and I took a taxi across London to his flat. I was quite emotional in the taxi. 'How could I have put myself in such a vulnerable situation?' I needed another drink to numb out the reality.

Tim gave me a big hug when I arrived and went to fetch some more wine. It was great to see his handsome, friendly face. A few glasses of wine later we kissed for the first time in ages. We then went up to bed. When I returned from the bathroom, having changed into one of his t-shirts, I found Tim already asleep. I climbed in beside him, aching to be kissed and held, but he was dead to the world. Once more, I felt rejected and alone.

The next morning I was so ill I was barely able to make the train journey home. In the cold, sober light of day I realised how unloving and untrue I had been to myself. It appeared I was still being 'co-dependent', that is, overly dependent on others to meet my needs, running and hiding from my feelings, being compliant and addicted to seeking emotional support and love from men rather than meeting my own needs. In addition, I was struggling to let go of my old life and identity. I couldn't believe how I had jeopardised my healing journey by overdoing the alcohol and the activity. I found it so uncomfortable to accept responsibility for my actions. In that moment, it was easier to blame my friend for 'making' me drink wine and for leaving me with the stranger. I was relieved to have a therapy session during the week to work through my feelings about each aspect of the experience, to learn from it and get back on track.

Shedding more layers

The therapy and self-help were slowly helping me heal my mind and emotions, but I was still severely lacking in energy. A fellow M.E. sufferer gave me a newspaper article on the subject which led me to explore alternative treatments including acupuncture and kinesiology. It also motivated me to seek advice from a qualified naturopath and nutritionist, who suggested I had some blood tests. Consequently, I discovered I also had Candida Albicans (a yeast overgrowth) and several food intolerances.

To assist my body to heal itself, the naturopath designed a special diet for me which involved excluding gluten, wheat, sugar, dairy, yeast, caffeine and a few other products. This meant no more alcohol or chocolate, for a while at least.

All my old comfort foods and emotional crutches were taken away from me. There really was no escape from myself and my emotions. Without these, especially a box of chocolates and a glass of wine when I was feeling low, I would no longer be able to bury my feelings, numb out or distract myself from the real causes of my unhappiness.

It was a shock. I felt even more exposed, vulnerable and socially unacceptable as, when I did manage to go out, I could only drink bottled water. By having what was at the time perceived as such an unusual diet I attracted attention to myself, which is something I hated because of my continuing low self-esteem. One month later, though, I had become accustomed to the lifestyle change, my energy levels had improved and some of the other symptoms had slightly abated. Nevertheless, a seed of doubt regarding my chances of finding true love with such a socially challenging lifestyle began to grow.

Awakening to my spirit

Up until now I had been concentrating on healing my mind and body. However, there was another aspect of myself that I was only just starting to wake up to – my spirit (see Secrets One, Two and Three). I read about it in Louise Hay's book *Life! Reflections on Your Journey*. Referring to this aspect of ourselves, she says: 'deep at the centre of our being there is an infinite well of love, an infinite well of joy, an infinite well of peace and an infinite well of wisdom'. She goes on to describe it as 'that part of you that is totally connected to all the wisdom in the universe' (p.90). I didn't really understand what she meant at first, but I was eager to discover more as it sounded wonderful.

I soon learnt that connecting with this aspect of myself didn't mean I had to conform to a specific set of rules or dogma, nor did I have to worship a particular God in a specific building in order to feel connected. Instead, I could practise quiet reflection, meditation, yoga or Tai chi to achieve this. I purchased a CD by Dr Wayne Dyer on how to meditate. This particular meditation involved saying 'Ah' out loud for 20 minutes, so as I was feeling a little self-conscious, I waited until my family were out each day before doing it! Once I got into the habit of it, I began to notice that I felt more loved and supported in the moments of conscious connection despite my continuing health issues. I found it helped me to feel a lot better. I felt calmer, more peaceful and a little more compassionate towards myself.

In addition, I discovered an alternative therapist who made house visits offering Reiki (see Other Resources), a form of hands-on spiritual healing whereby the practitioner channels what is referred to as Universal Life Force Energy. The treatments felt wonderfully nurturing and healing and had a profound effect on me. The Reiki also helped me to feel more connected to my spirit, and so when I felt well enough I trained to be a Reiki practitioner. Once trained, I was able to nurture myself using Reiki. It was during my Reiki training that I discovered more about the Universe, or cosmos, and the support it can offer us in creating our desires (see Secrets Five, Six and Seven). It was also the place I first found out about angels, but that's another story!

Making my heart sing

During one of my therapy sessions, the therapist introduced me to another important aspect of myself that I had been unaware of previously: that is, my childlike self or 'Inner Child' (see Secret Four for more on the Inner Child). Through the therapy, I learnt to recognise that I had been neglecting to make time for any healthy, childlike fun in my life. In the past, when I hadn't been working, I had been searching for true love or trying to numb out through the lack of it. More recently, I had been focusing on curing myself of M.E., yet I had been unaware of how important it is for health and happiness to make time for genuine fun.

I spent time reflecting on the happy times in my childhood and what I had liked to do. I remembered I had loved singing and taking part in school performances. I did some research and found that my local adult college was offering an evening course in Musical Theatre once a week. The following Monday, I nervously went along to my first class.

There were about ten people in the group, most of whom were men. They were really great guys: however, they were gay. 'I obviously won't find The One here!' I thought to myself. But I had such fun doing the group and the individual singing, and as the course progressed a little bit of acting too, that it wasn't long before it no longer mattered to me. I found that my confidence and self-esteem were increasing as a result of taking part and that was giving me great pleasure in itself. I felt uplifted, carefree and youthful. It gave me a new sense of joy and lightness of being. It really felt as though my heart was singing (see Secret Four).

By doing the classes, I discovered what healthy fun activities can feel like, how much longer-lasting their benefits are, and the fact that they do not have unwanted, potentially damaging side-effects, unlike my old 'fun' pastimes: drinking, partying and pulling strangers! After a few weeks, I was experiencing more energy and feeling happier, so much so that I decided to stop therapy.

A new start

Finally, September and the first day of university arrived. Despite the doctor's original prognosis I was overjoyed to feel well enough to start the course. I still needed to rest a great deal, and some days were better than others. But it was my opportunity to finally start to feel good enough and as intelligent as people like John. I was determined to give it my best shot.

However as I made the long journey from my parents' house to university, I was full of anxiety. 'Will I be able to cope with doing this journey regularly? Will I be able to manage the workload? Will the other students accept me with my dietary and energy challenges?' I wound myself up into such a state about it, a sign that I had a way to go before I was really healed.

Similarly, although I had made some personal changes and a level of healing had occurred within me, I continued to seek love outside of myself. Consequently, when I found the hall for our first session of the day, I looked around the room to see if The One might be there. I doubted he was, as 80 per cent of the group were women. Those that were male appeared to be about 20 years old – the same age as my brother. Much too young for me!

There were plenty of opportunities outside of the course to socialise and meet guys, particularly in the student bar, but I didn't have the energy for it. At least I had started the three-year Psychology and Counselling course. My dream was turning into reality. 'Maybe one day I will find true love too?' I continued to live in hope.

CHAPTER 10

Alex – almost The One

A return to therapy

One month on, despite the progress I'd made, being at university evoked some unhealed emotions. Once more, I felt as though I was between two worlds. I missed aspects of my old life, particularly being able to socialise properly. However, I knew that my old life wouldn't lead me to what I wanted: well-being, a fulfilling career, true love and happiness. But I longed to feel 'normal', that I belonged.

The majority of my university peers were 18 to 21 years old. Being around them made me highly conscious that I was getting older and in increasing danger of being left on the shelf. Not a day went by when I didn't think about men and finding The One. Somehow I had fallen off the path again on my journey of transformation. I had to take action to change it if I was ever to find lasting happiness.

The problem was that I didn't know myself well enough yet to see what I could do to change the way I felt. I regretted my decision to end therapy. I missed having someone who understood me. I missed the support and the insights to help me change and move forward. I didn't feel comfortable opening up to my new university friends. I was also doubtful they could help me to change. A few weeks later, determined to continue moving forwards, I returned to therapy.

Asking the universe for help

When I wasn't studying, I continued to invest time and energy in knowing myself better, loving myself more, being true to myself and making my heart sing as often as possible (see Secrets One, Two, Three and Four). Through all the self-help books I was reading and the work I was doing in therapy, I discovered the importance of knowing what you want in terms of a partner and a relationship and asking for it (see Secret Five). Prior to this, I had never thought about what I wanted beyond the surface level. I had gained a little insight following my experiences with Harry and John, but I had never really thought about the qualities I wanted the person to have, or what a true love relationship would actually look like for me. I had never written down the few thoughts I had about what I wanted, nor asked the Universe for help.

As nothing I had previously done had worked, I was determined to try something new. I spent time reflecting on my past relationships and on what I'd learnt on my journey thus far to help me clarify what I wanted. I then wrote my first celestial advert (see Secret Five). I wanted a kind, funny, honest, trustworthy, loving, intelligent, generous, spiritually minded and supportive guy who I was attracted to. I knew that I wanted someone who was interested in healthy eating and taking care of himself. I focused on the qualities, not on looks. I included finding them attractive as I knew that was important, but I left what they looked like up to the Universe.

I wrote down what I wanted in my personal diary in the form of an advert. I wrote it in the present tense, saying such things as 'My partner is kind. My partner is interested in healthy eating and takes care of himself. I find my partner attractive . . .'. and so on. Unlike traditional adverts, this one would remain in my diary. It was just between the Universe and myself.

In writing the celestial advert I was consciously asking the Universe to send me this person when the time was right. In the meantime I would commit to doing my part of the process. I would indelibly etch the contents of the advert in my mind and I would work on recognising and connecting with these qualities in myself and on becoming The One myself (see Secret Six). Less than two months later I experienced a significant moment of synchronicity.

A synchronistic article

As I didn't want to attract sympathy or be treated any differently from other students, very few people on my course knew that I was healing myself of M.E. One woman I had told happened to be reading a copy of a national student psychology magazine, when she came across an article entitled 'The life of a student with M.E.' by an Alex Howard, from Swansea University. She gave me the article, thinking that it might be of interest to me.

I found a quiet place in the library to read it. As I read the article, I felt deeply moved. This Alex person was someone who, without knowing me at all, understood exactly what I was going through. They described perfectly the feelings and experiences I was having trying simultaneously to heal myself from M.E. and do a full-time degree course. The more I read, the more I cried with relief. It felt like a message sent from heaven.

Alex had included an email address at the end of the article for any readers requiring further information. I wanted to thank Alex for being brave enough to share their story and for the realisation that I wasn't alone in my challenging experience. There was no clue in the article as to Alex's gender. It was irrelevant to me, though. I hoped we could support each other over the internet as we worked through our degree courses, and in particular share healing methods. 'Besides,' I thought, 'even if Alex turns out to be male, the fact that they are doing a degree in Wales makes it virtually impossible for us to establish and sustain a relationship. Long-distance relationships never work for me.'

I found it quite difficult writing the email to Alex as it was the first time, outside of therapy, that I was so open and honest with another person about my feelings and experiences. I felt very anxious as I waited for Alex to reply and give their reaction to what I'd shared. Thankfully the reply was very positive and I discovered a kindred spirit in cyberspace.

My new e-pal

It transpired that Alex was male after all and the article was taken from a book he was writing about his healing journey (entitled *Why ME?* – now published). Discovering that Alex was male affected me. His article had resonated with me greatly. We had a lot in common and I started to wonder if there was any chance of romance. As I had yet to let go of the addictive behaviour pattern of consciously looking for true love outside myself, I even wondered if he could be The One.

Nevertheless, my hopes were crushed when, after reading a few more chapters of his book, I discovered he was only 20 years old. Having just turned 31, I felt it would be too weird for me and would never work. I was quick to remind myself that I needed a supportive platonic friend who understood what I was going through. I did not need a 'Toy Boy'!

I discovered intimate details about Alex's life as I read the chapters he emailed to me. I was deeply moved by the courage, honesty and maturity that came across in his writing. He seemed like an amazing guy who'd been through a lot already in his life. He was into self-development and matters relating to what is known as the field of 'Mind, Body and Spirit', and had even studied Reiki. Alex appeared to be a most untypical 20-year-old and we had developed a good friendship by the end of my first term at university.

Alex told me he was coming to London for part of the Christmas holidays. We were both keen to meet up and share our experiences. The night before we were due to meet, Alex phoned to confirm the arrangements. We spoke for over an hour. As I listened to his voice I was surprised to find it very sexy. It wasn't what I expected him to sound like at his age. I noticed I now had butterflies in my stomach about meeting him. Nevertheless I didn't want to get my hopes up. Even if I could cope with the age difference, I was probably far too old for him.

Meeting Alex

Alex had offered to cook me dinner at his uncle's flat in London, as he had the place to himself for the weekend. We arranged to meet at the tube station. It was easy to recognise Alex as he was just as he had described, except even better looking. I knew I would have to keep my feelings in check to prevent myself from getting carried away with any romantic fantasies. Being so much younger than me he surely couldn't be The One.

Alex greeted me with a friendly hug and we made our way to the flat. We talked virtually non-stop, barely finding the time to cook and eat dinner. We had so much in common. Even our diets were virtually the same. We connected on a deep level; I felt as though I had known Alex for ages. The matter of his age faded into the background. The evening flew by and suddenly it was time for me to go. But I didn't want to leave. It was already quite late and since having M.E. I felt more vulnerable travelling on public transport after dark. I was also enjoying being with Alex so much that I didn't want it to end. It was wonderful for me to be with a guy who listened, openly shared his feelings and was heterosexual!

Although I wanted to stay, I didn't want to have sex with Alex nor did I want to mislead him. I explained this to him. He understood and was totally accepting. He valued our friendship as much as I did. It was a relief. Nevertheless, the flat was cold and due to the lack of furniture and bedding, we would have to share the bed. In the early hours of the morning, as I lay next to Alex, we cuddled trying to keep warm. It had been such a lovely evening and I felt so close to him in many ways that I found I had the desire to kiss him. He kissed me back. The connection between us was amazing. There was something very special about Alex and I hoped we would spend more time together.

Dating in the awake zone

The following day, Alex asked me out on a date. First I had to go home and change my clothes and get some rest as I was worried about the effect that such little sleep would have on my health. Later, as we walked to the cinema that night, Alex held my hand and, despite the 11-year age gap, I thought we looked quite good when I saw our reflection in a shop window. After the film neither of us wanted to part, particularly as Alex was heading back to Wales later that week. I had an urge to invite him to stay with me at my parents' house. And so after clearing it with them, which felt so bizarre considering I was 31, I invited him back.

It was unusually comfortable being with Alex at my parents'. He felt like part of the family straight away. I also liked the innocence and the lightness of our relationship. It was like a breath of fresh air following all the heavy emotional dramas I'd experienced in my search for true love over the years. What Alex and I had together was very different from anything I had ever experienced before. 'Could he be The One?' I wondered.

Taking it to the next level

In the early stages of our getting to know each other, I shared intimate details of myself and my life with Alex as he did with me. It was great to have an open and honest relationship, but it also meant that I felt more vulnerable and sensitive than I had ever felt when dating. Consequently it took some time before I felt ready to take our relationship to the next level. Yet I still felt cherished, loved and wanted. Alex never tried to put pressure on me. I believe this was partly down to the fact that I was now being true to myself (see Secret Three), in addition to Alex being the respectful person he is.

And, despite the age difference, we had common values and dreams. We were both doing whatever it took to heal ourselves of M.E., also exploring spirituality and personal growth and having fun whenever we had the energy. When we eventually had sex, I discovered the connection Alex and I had as friends spilled over into our love-making. Being with Alex was wonderful. 'Is this what true love looks like?' I wondered.

However, as a result of taking our relationship to the next level, we created new challenges for ourselves. Whenever I went to stay with Alex in Wales, we both expected to make love. The problem was that it wasn't often that we both had the energy at the same time. In the past this could have signalled the end, but because we had a very authentic relationship, both being committed to being true to ourselves, rather than blame each other we took responsibility for our own feelings, supported each other and worked through it.

A breakthrough

Following our end-of-year exams, Alex and I went on holiday together. We took around six Mind, Body and Spirit books with us in the hope of learning something that could help us move further forward in our healing. It led to a significant breakthrough. One of the books was about Neuro-Linguistic Programming, or NLP (see Further Reading). Alex was so intrigued about the healing benefits of NLP described in the book that when he returned to the UK he located an NLP practitioner and booked a series of sessions. He experienced such great benefit from them that he decided to do the NLP practitioner training himself, while completing the final year of his degree.

I had yet to be convinced about NLP. I was focused on getting through the second year of my degree. I had been warned to expect an increased workload and had moved into the Halls of Residence so I didn't have to make the long journey from my parents' house any more. I hoped it would help reduce the stress. However, I still had to complete the massage course I had been doing over the university holidays. Now I felt that I was putting myself under too much pressure, but at least there were only a few weeks left of the massage course.

Aside from the workload, I had to manage my emotions regarding my relationship with Alex. He would graduate in the summer and I knew that things would change. We had been open and honest with each other about our desires for the future. Alex had expressed his lack of desire to settle down, as he naturally wanted to experience more of life; I, on the other hand, thought I was ready to. Although we talked openly, we were unable to resolve the matter. After over a year of being together, our ages and the different stages we were at in our lives had become an issue.

Reaching a new level of self-awareness and honesty

I felt myself pushing Alex away emotionally and physically, unconsciously trying to protect myself from getting hurt. A voice in my head was telling me that Alex was not right for me and that I should keep my options open. It was trying to convince me to be free again so I could experience the wonders of attracting someone new, the thrill of the chase and then the challenge of maintaining their interest.

Turning to Tim

I resorted to past behaviour and contacted Tim. We went out for dinner. This time I did not drink any alcohol: I kept to my commitment and watched instead as Tim proceeded to drink. In my sober state and with my increased awareness, I was able to perceive the truth more clearly. I noticed that Tim withheld his feelings from me, until the effects of the alcohol took hold. He also then became much more tactile and open. It was a very curious experience to watch the changes in him the more he drank. I recognised that it was how I used to be.

By the end of the night Tim said we should make a pact. If neither of us was married by the time we were 40, we should marry each other. In the past this would have been music to my ears. Now, though, I knew it would be settling for second best and co-dependency because, although we were still friends, our interests, values and outlooks on life had become very different. There was no romance or chemistry there either. I finally had enough awareness and self-love to let go of Tim emotionally, once and for all.

Afterwards I spent time quietly reflecting on my thoughts and feelings. I realised that the thoughts about finding someone else were just messages from my ego, the voice of fear, about my not being good enough, a belief that plagued me repeatedly. The fearful part of me believed I needed 'new' men, new relationships to prove to myself that this belief was untrue. It was a self-sabotaging pattern, a block keeping me away from true love.

I wanted to work on the 'not feeling good enough' belief as it was also affecting my healing progress. I decided to try *The Journey*® process by Brandon Bays (see Bibliography). Alex kindly offered to guide me through it. I found the experience very profound and incredibly powerful. It helped me to release a lot of negative emotional blocks. Although I did feel better about myself, I had not yet managed to change the belief entirely. Nevertheless, the process had a major impact on my relationship with Alex.

Becoming just good friends

Following the release of the emotional baggage and other psychological aspects of the process, I knew I didn't want to be in a relationship with Alex any more. I felt that I'd changed – as though I had grown up emotionally. I now wanted something different. I felt ready for a man my own age. I believed I was ready to commit. Although Alex was a wonderful guy, I no longer perceived him as a lover or a potential husband, but rather a good friend. Because of all the changes I had made on my inner journey, I was able to end our relationship in a kind, loving and truthful way. I felt amazingly liberated as I had the courage to speak openly and honestly to Alex, face to face. As a result our friendship lasts to this day.

Alex was not The One, but he was the closest thing to it I had ever experienced. Finally, I had a good idea of what true love looked like and felt like. I devised a new celestial advert, asked the Universe for what I wanted and set about becoming The One myself.

CHAPTER 11

Single and content, eventually

The immediate high . . .

Following the break-up with Alex I did not feel a sense
of loss. There was no ache or longing to be with someone, just nice memories of the wonderful time we had
spent together. I knew it was no coincidence that I had
attracted someone like Alex to me. He had been visible proof
that I had radically improved the relationship I had with
myself, and that gave me great personal satisfaction.

. . . Followed by the low

Nevertheless, just as Alex hadn't been The One completely,
I wasn't fully content with myself. I had yet to cure myself of
M.E. and was feeling increasingly frustrated. I had tried
many alternative therapies and read so many books on healing and self-development. I was running out of ideas and
patience with my body.

It had been less of an issue when I was dating Alex as,
being in a similar position himself, he had been very understanding. Now single again, I was acutely aware of my
situation. I would be 33 years old in October. Some of my
university friends in their twenties were in serious relation-

ships. In my low moments, I was still afraid I wouldn't find The One and would be left, alone, on the shelf.

A month or so later, there was a Psychic Fair at my local leisure centre. I went along and decided to have a 30-minute psychic reading. I was a little nervous, but the male psychic I felt drawn to had some positive testimonials. I felt I was in safe hands. I was desperate for some answers: the fearful, impatient part of me needed to know when I would be fully recovered from M.E. and when I would meet The One.

I didn't give the psychic any information about myself. First I asked him about my health. He knew so much and described exactly what I had been going through. It was as though he had been watching over me for the last couple of years, witnessing my journey. Although he was spot-on about the past and the present and his empathy was comforting, he couldn't tell me what I really wanted to know, what would happen in the future. He gave a very vague response, something about it all coming right in the end. I moved on to my next question.

I asked the psychic if he could tell me when I'd meet The One. 'You'll meet someone around the end of October or beginning of November this year', he replied. That was six months away. I felt gutted to hear I had to wait that long after all the work I had done on myself. 'Are you sure it won't be before then?' I asked, urging him to check again. 'No. That's what my guides are telling me', he confirmed. My heart sank. He shared some other minor details and then my time was up.

I left the leisure centre feeling very disheartened. From everything I had learnt, coupled with an increased self-awareness, I knew that if I had totally improved the relationship with myself, the state of my health and being single would not affect my happiness the way that it was doing. I realised that somehow I had slipped off the path and had taken a few steps backwards once more.

I decided to turn inwards and spend some time reflecting more deeply on what was really going on for me, especially on what had caused me to react to the psychic's news in such a way. I became aware that I was feeling desperate and needy. I was continuing to look for love and happiness in the wrong place. I took a good look at what was going on in my life, where I was investing my time and my thoughts.

I realised that I had been focusing on what I perceived as the negative aspects of my health, such as the fact that my energy levels continued to fluctuate and I needed to rest completely one day a week. I had also been focusing on the aspects of my diet that I found frustrating. I had been focusing on what I *didn't* want in my life. No wonder I wasn't happy! I knew that this had to change. I had to start focusing on the positive aspects of my health, including having had enough energy in the last year to do a degree and at the same time train as a massage therapist. I needed to focus on the fact that the university canteen did at least have jacket potatoes so there was something hot I could eat! I needed to remember that I had also been able to sustain a loving, long-distance relationship for over a year.

After a while, I recognised another familiar pattern. I had continued on some level to 'need' a man to make me feel loved and happy rather than being fully focused on becoming The One myself (see Secret Six). I hadn't been spending enough time on making myself happy. At least this time, though, I had been fulfilling my intellectual and physical needs, unlike before, which gave me further proof that I had made some significant progress.

Alex and I were (and continue to be) passionate about working on ourselves not only mentally and physically but emotionally and spiritually too. I missed being around someone who had the same interests and the same level of passion and commitment. We had had a lot of fun together, too, during our relationship. Now, although it was the university holidays, I was spending time working on my third-year dissertation in the hope of getting a head start and thus reducing my stress during the last year of the course. I also had some Reiki and massage clients. I was not making any time for genuine, healthy fun. After discovering her existence only recently, I was already neglecting my 'Inner Child' once more and, consequently, my heart wasn't singing at all. I chose to re-address this imbalance.

A divine discovery

'Perhaps a day in central London would be fun?' I thought to myself. I decided to give it a try – forgetting that it was the day of the Queen Mother's funeral! I got out at Piccadilly Circus. It seemed quieter than usual. It was strange. Then I noticed there were signs on the shop windows stating that businesses would be observing a few minutes' silence out of respect for the Queen Mum – and then I remembered what day it was. 'Not a great day for fun then!' I realised. Nonetheless, it did feel a day for a spiritual connection of a different kind and I had the urge to be in a church to observe the silence. I remembered that St. James' church was close, as my old office was nearby. I used to be a regular visitor to the café next to the church, but in all my years in London I had never entered the church building before.

As I was walking out of the church after observing the silence, a booklet entitled *Alternatives*, located in a rack against the wall, caught my eye. I assumed it was promoting the activities of the church and, not being religious myself, I dismissed it automatically and walked outside. However, my intuition urged me to go back into the church and pick it up. I followed the guidance and collected the booklet. I read that 'Alternatives' (see Other Resources) is a non-profit organisation which regularly hosts inspiring, educational and fun talks and workshops for the mind, emotions, body and spirit. The church just happened to be the location of the head office and the venue for the Monday evening events. It was exactly what I needed. It seemed to be heaven-sent, especially when I later read that Alternatives had been holding events in St James' church for over 20 years and I had never noticed it before!

I started to attend the Monday evening talks. Not only were they very informative and inspirational in themselves, but the evenings also gave me the opportunity to meet and talk to other like-minded people. After a few weeks, I was enjoying the evenings so much that I became part of the Alternatives volunteer team helping with the running of the talks and workshops. I was now part of a group of people passionate about the field of Mind, Body and Spirit, especially connecting with their true selves and having childlike fun. I loved volunteering, giving something back to help this amazing organisation. My heart was singing once more.

Another heaven-sent book

I also continued to reflect on the emotional and behavioural patterns I had yet to heal in order to further improve the relationship with myself. 'So many books have helped me on my journey. I wonder if there's a book that can help me now', I pondered. I went to my local bookshop to find out. As usual, I wandered around the self-help section. Nothing I picked off the shelf hit the spot for me so I decided to leave. As I was walking towards the door, I suddenly noticed a book called *The Surrendered Single* by Laura Doyle (see Bibliography). The title didn't resonate with me at all, but my intuition was nudging me to flick through it. I know the importance of listening to my intuition and so I purchased it. The book turned out to be exactly what I needed as it helped me to gain some insights into my issues and provided some practical steps that I could take in order to move forward.

Experiencing the power of forgiveness

A few weeks later my brother paid me an unexpected visit. He wanted to talk to me as his steady girlfriend, Anne, had just ended their relationship. He was devastated. They had got together while they were living with their respective parents, five minutes away from each other. Some months later, Anne began her degree at a university four hours' drive away. The distance took its toll on the relationship. I knew Anne and her family background well. It appeared she was making the most of her new-found freedom after years of rigid parental control. In contrast, nothing had changed in my brother's life.

As I listened to my brother pouring his heart out, I had a flashback to my break-up with Ben. The situation was virtually identical. I could totally understand what had been going on for Anne but it was extremely painful to see my brother so distraught. Suddenly I realised what it must have felt like for Ben. The fact that I agreed to go to the dinner and dance with him and share a bed, even though the relationship had finished as far as I was concerned, must have confused and hurt him. I realised I had not forgiven myself for the way I had ended it. But it wasn't too late to do something about it. I needed to know that Ben was OK. I needed to know that the experience with me hadn't put him off relationships for life.

I set about finding Ben. I called the last place I knew he worked at; they told me he'd left several years previously but were kind enough to let me know where he moved on to. Several calls later, I managed to locate his current company. He was still in retail. Although I didn't know which store he worked at, I knew the number for the head office and contacted them. 'I'm sorry but we're not permitted to give out that information' was the reply. 'I really need to get hold of him. Is there anything else I can do?' I asked, desperate to contact Ben. 'Well, if you email us your details, we will forward them on to him.' I did as I was instructed. However, I was doubtful Ben would contact me. It had been 13 years since we last spoke to each other. I also hoped he wouldn't get the wrong idea and think that I wanted a relationship with him again. I was taking a big risk, but it felt the right thing to do.

A few days later the phone rang. I answered. It was Ben. He sounded exactly the same, despite the passing of time. I was so relieved he called. Finally, I had the opportunity to make amends. I explained in some detail why I had tracked him down after all this time. When I finished explaining, he told me that although he had been affected by the break-up for a while, he had taken the opportunity to spread his wings and make a new life for himself away from home. He also said it hadn't put him off relationships either. He was actually happily married and about to become a father. At the end of our conversation, Ben asked if I was married. I admitted The One hadn't appeared in my life yet. He wished me luck in finding him and I wished him all the best with being a Dad.

I sat and quietly reflected on the conversation afterwards. I felt such a huge sense of relief. I also felt more at peace with myself. It was as though something quite magical had occurred, as though a spell had been broken. It helped me to understand how hard I was on myself about things I had done in the past and that others had moved on from. The person I had been hurting the most was me. Realising that this had been having a detrimental effect on the relationship with myself, I felt motivated to do more unresolved forgiveness work (see Secret Two).

Rebalancing my masculine and feminine sides

Although I was making great progress, further reading and Chinese medicine led me to discover that I continued to have an imbalance in my life. I grew up, like many people, in a household where working and keeping busy were encouraged from a young age, whereas resting and nurturing oneself were not, unless you were ill. Therefore, I had always been more comfortable with my masculine side (the 'Yang'), the driven part of me which exerts its power through activity and control. I used to perceive the receptive, nurturing, feminine part of myself (the 'Yin') as rather weak.

It appeared that to be healthy and happy I had to rebalance my masculine and feminine forces, the Yin and Yang. I committed to increasing my conscious awareness of when my masculine side was trying to dominate me by pushing me too hard and wanting to control everything. Then, I did what I could to change the behaviour and do things in moderation and learn to let go more. I committed to investing more time and energy in being kinder to myself, to nurturing and pampering myself, and to viewing it as a strength rather than a weakness. I also started to wear clothes that I felt more feminine in.

Transformational healing occurs

I spoke to Alex about my recent discoveries and about my increased determination to heal myself of M.E. and improve the relationship with myself even further. He recommended I have some NLP and hypnotherapy sessions. The first two sessions were very helpful. I gained a greater understanding of my issues and what patterns I was running to cause them, and I learnt techniques to change them. The third session, though, was transformational. At the end of it, I felt completely full of energy, like I hadn't felt in years. My head was clear. All my symptoms had gone. I felt as though I had been set free. It was the last piece in my healing jigsaw puzzle. After two and a half years I finally felt healed of M.E.

Finding true love at last

September had arrived. My self-esteem was higher than it had ever been. I felt empowered. I was feeding myself loving thoughts, I was speaking positively about myself, I was treating my body with kindness, nurturing it, giving it healthy, nutritious food, doing gentle exercise and pampering it. I had more control over my emotions. I was feeling good about myself and following it through with actions by ensuring I remained true to myself at all times. I was making time to quietly reflect, to meditate and give myself Reiki. In addition, I was regularly attending to the needs of my Inner Child, doing fun childlike things and making my heart sing with such activities as volunteering at Alternatives.

I didn't care about what the psychic had predicted months previously. I had stopped feeling like a social misfit through being single and was no longer controlled by fearful thoughts that I would be left on the shelf. I had stopped looking. I was genuinely enjoying my life. I had *let go* (see

Secret Seven). I could feel the difference emotionally and physically. Whenever my Mum or my friends told me about someone I knew who was getting married, I didn't dissolve into tears, nor did I have a sinking feeling in the pit of my stomach. I no longer felt angry, rejected or unwanted because I was nowhere near getting married. Instead I felt genuine joy and happiness for the person.

I was finally feeling happy, complete and at peace with myself. I had overcome my addiction to seeking love outside of myself and my co-dependence. I had reached a place of deep knowing that I was a woman who felt loved, loving and lovable. I had been through a lot and I had made it. I had created my happiness. I had discovered, and consciously connected with, my true self. It had led me to find true love in the place I had least expected, within myself. It was a great place to be.

CHAPTER 12

Mark – The One

A life-changing course

Having personally benefited from the sessions of NLP and wanting to be better equipped to assist others to change, I decided to follow in Alex's footsteps and do the NLP diploma while completing the final year of my degree. Alex had coped well with the workload, especially considering he had sustained a long-distance relationship with me and had been continuing to try and heal from M.E. at the same time. I was well again – and had only a loving relationship with myself to sustain. I could definitely do both courses.

Just a few weeks of the university holidays remained. I made the most of the free time and went on holiday to France with my family. I returned feeling very relaxed and rejuvenated and eager to start the NLP course.

The first of the ten weekends of the NLP diploma was upon me. I was really excited about learning the new theories and techniques. I found myself a seat in the classroom. When everyone had arrived, we were asked to introduce ourselves. Out of habit I scanned the group, casually checking to see if The One might be present. I looked at the men's faces first and then their ring fingers! I didn't feel drawn to any of the seemingly single men. This time, though, I felt totally calm about it. Rather than being disappointed as I had in the past, my new sense of completeness and happiness meant I felt at peace. It was another joyful reminder that I had improved the relationship with myself. The course itself was incredibly thought-provoking and stimulating. We even had volunteer clients to work with on the Sunday. We were kept so busy that the weekend was over in no time.

A life-defining decision

I soon returned to university. It wasn't long before my new thoughts and behaviours were severely tested as the work started to pile up. Three weeks later, I felt overwhelmed by the amount of university course work. I hadn't completed my NLP homework and I was meant to spend the coming weekend on the course. I couldn't face it. I needed a rest, not more work. I had thought I could do both courses and continue to fulfil all my emotional, physical and spiritual needs. It seemed I had asked too much of myself. Determined to honour my commitment to being truly nurturing and loving to myself, I realised I had to withdraw from the NLP diploma.

I phoned the course Director and explained what was going on. I felt very upset. I had to find out if there was another way. 'Can I defer for a year?' I asked, thinking that might work. 'No. That's not possible', he replied. The course fee was a lot of money to me. Although I was desperate to restore my inner peace and happiness, I didn't want to throw nearly £2,000 down the drain. 'But, if I drop out, will you give me a refund?' 'No' came his reply once more. 'How could he do this to me?' I cried to myself as I slipped into victim mode. 'He's being so unfair. Why doesn't he understand what I'm going through?'

The Director remained detached from his emotions and gave me some NLP and coaching on the phone to help me with my stress and overwhelmed patterns instead. He also assured me I would receive extra support for the remaining nine weekends of the diploma from the coaches and my peers. I subsequently chose to carry on doing both courses.

Meeting The One

A few days later, the second NLP weekend arrived. Now on a gluten-free diet, I made sure I prepared enough healthy and gluten-free food to last me for the day. I also focused on warmth and comfort rather than style when getting dressed as the weather had turned cold and I wanted to be kind to myself. Hence, unlike in the past, despite the demands on my time, I continued to support myself and fulfil my needs.

I made the hour and a half journey to the school in North London and arrived in time to hear an announcement by the Director. 'I've now changed my policy with regards to allowing students to join the course beyond the first weekend. So, two new people have joined the group today, Mark and Fi.' Mark introduced himself and said a few words. He looked about 45 years old and was quite tall, but chunky with it. He came across as a very nice, friendly and funny guy.

When the morning break arrived, I went over to browse through the books the Director was selling. Mark joined me. He asked me why I was doing the diploma. I shared my reasons. 'And you?' I asked in return. 'I'm at a crossroads in my life in terms of my career and my relationship. I've been working in computing for many years but my heart lies in helping people change', he explained.

'In terms of my relationship, my heart's not in that either', he confessed, adding that he could see no future in it. He told me he was procrastinating. He said he hoped the course would help him resolve both issues. Mark went on to explain that he was living by himself in Wales during the week due to his work contract and wasn't spending much time at all with his partner at the house they shared in the South of England. I was amazed he had chosen to do this particular NLP course in North London when he was dividing his time between Wales and the South of England. It involved a great deal of travelling, but the Universe works in mysterious ways!

Throughout the course that Saturday, I received all the support I was promised. I even had fun, especially with Mark. He made me laugh a lot when we paired up to practice the techniques we'd learnt. The day passed very quickly and we were soon making our respective ways home.

I considered what a lovely guy Mark was as I walked to the bus stop that evening. He was mature, intelligent, open, honest, warm and kind but also very funny too. I pondered his dilemma concerning his relationship. He had said he knew his partner wasn't The One. He was choosing to stay in the relationship despite being discontented. It sounded very familiar and reminded me of my own past. 'He's not being fair or loving to himself or his girlfriend', I thought to myself.

Approaching the bus stop I noticed Mark was still waiting. I felt really happy to see him. We talked while waiting for the bus and the conversation flowed naturally. I found out his real age: he was actually 37 not 45. He joked that he had his divorce to thank for his prematurely grey hair! During the journey to the station, our level of conversation deepened. We were being very open with each other and I took the opportunity to share my observation about him appearing to be settling for second best, for a relationship with The Other rather than The One. He wasn't offended. 'I know you're right. I've got a lot to think about', he admitted. We then said goodbye and went our separate ways.

The moment I knew

I thought about Mark a great deal that night. He had made a deep impression on me. I felt there was a connection between us on some level. I looked forward to seeing him the following day.

But on Sunday morning, I awoke to discover that high winds had battered the country overnight and there were problems on the trains. I wasn't sure Mark would be able to make the long train journey to North London. I managed to get to the school, although it took a while. The time went by and there was still no sign of Mark. With only one hour of the course remaining, Mark finally arrived. He caught up as much as possible. Then it was time to leave once more. 'Are you heading to the bus stop again today?' Mark asked. 'Yes', I answered. 'Then I'll walk with you, if that's OK?' I was flattered. We were so deep in conversation that when we got to the bus stop we decided to carry on walking all the way to the train station. En route, I needed to stop off at the supermarket to buy my 'roast dinner for one'. Mark said he'd buy himself a sandwich.

Inside the supermarket Mark went off to find his sandwich while I went to locate my dinner. Having found what I needed, I went in search of Mark. As I turned into the sandwich aisle, I spotted him at the opposite end. He was facing me. Suddenly it was as though time stood still. I was rooted to the spot. I was seeing a vision. I could see myself contentedly washing Mark's socks in the kitchen sink! It was bizarre. Accompanying the vision was a deep feeling, a *knowing*, that I was facing The One. There was not a single doubt in any part of my being. The vision disappeared as suddenly as it had appeared. I was back in reality. Nevertheless, the deep feeling, the knowing, remained. I knew that someday I was going to marry Mark. I didn't know when, though, and I was totally relaxed about it. I chose to keep my vision to myself and we continued on to the station.

Divine intervention

We arrived to find that the trains had temporarily stopped running because of the bad weather. 'Do you fancy a drink in the pub while we wait for our trains?' Mark asked. 'Sounds like a good idea to me', I replied. I found us a table while Mark went off to fetch some drinks. When he returned from the bar, he enquired about my unusual diet. He wanted to know everything about it and me. I opened up to him about my constant external search for love in the past, the burnout, my inner journey and my interest in the field of Mind, Body and Spirit. I trusted him enough to tell him I had been in therapy.

Mark was equally open about his own life, sharing that he too had experienced therapy, and that it had helped him find the strength to leave his unhappy marriage. He shared that he had also developed a different perspective on life during and since his divorce. It sounded as though he had experienced many other challenges throughout his life. The more we talked, the more we discovered we had in common. We had a deep connection and at the same time we had a great laugh together. Three hours later, the trains to my town were running again. It was time for me to leave. Mark walked me to the platform.

A changed person

A part of me wanted to invite Mark back to my place. Another part of me didn't. I loved his company and was reluctant to leave. But, I didn't want to ruin the day by being hasty and inviting him back, even if it was to sleep on the sofa. I knew it would have been too intimate too soon, especially as he was still in a relationship. I was not in a hurry. I was very happy as I was, plus I knew he was The One.

From that moment on, Mark and I developed a long-distance friendship over the phone and internet. He called me from Wales nearly every night. We talked for hours and never seemed to run out of things to say. Nevertheless, some three weeks later, I felt I could not continue our friendship outside of the NLP course any longer. We were getting on so well that I was finding it hard to remain detached emotionally (see Secret Seven). I felt that I wasn't being true to myself maintaining such a friendship. I couldn't allow myself to feel happy and excited about us while he was involved with someone else. It didn't feel right. Mark was disappointed but said that he understood.

Our first kiss

My intention had been to be true to myself and clear my conscience. However, the action proved to be a motivational spur for Mark. A few days later, he ended his relationship. When he phoned to ask if he could see me, I needed to be sure that he had withdrawn emotionally from his ex-partner. As he reminded me, although he had cared about her, he had known early on in the relationship that it had no future.

On the phone, Mark asked me if I envisaged him in my future. My supermarket vision flashed into my mind. I stayed silent. 'I take it that means yes, then', said Mark. 'I do too', he admitted. Wow! Things were moving fast. It felt natural and exciting, though. Nonetheless, I was staying with my parents that weekend and had hurt my leg; I was in some pain and unable to go out. 'I'd like to see you, but you'll have to come to my parents' house – and they will be in!' I warned him. I wasn't sure how a divorcee with teenage children would feel about meeting the parents so soon. It didn't dissuade him, though, and a few hours later he arrived.

During the evening we looked into each other's eyes as we talked across the dining room table. I felt an incredible chemistry flowing between us for the first time. Then, all too soon, it was time to say goodbye. Standing in the porch, Mark gave me a loving hug. It felt wonderful to be that close to him. It was Bonfire Night, and as we stood there listening to the fireworks going off Mark lowered his face to meet mine and tenderly kissed me. The kiss felt so powerful. It was like nothing I'd ever experienced before. It felt like fireworks were going off inside me too! I was in heaven. I had been truly content with myself and my life before I met Mark, but this added another dimension to it.

A true love relationship

Our first dinner date followed shortly afterwards. We got on really well and had great fun. It felt as though we had known each other for years rather than a few short weeks. We had several more dinner dates, with great deep, meaningful and honest conversations on many subjects and laughed a great deal. It wasn't long before we felt ready to take our relationship to the next level. It was another amazing experience and our love and connection deepened even further.

As the weeks passed, I discovered how amazingly thoughtful and considerate Mark is. He would often make the three-hour drive from Wales to my place to surprise me. He was incredibly supportive, doing whatever he could to help me each weekend of the NLP course when my workload doubled. I felt cherished and loved. It was wonderful to have such an authentic, open and honest relationship too. My previous relationships (excluding the one with Alex) had been far removed from what I now felt to be true love with another. It mirrored the journey of the relationship with myself.

The marriage proposal

Six weeks after our first kiss Mark invited me to his company's Christmas Ball, a formal affair at a luxury hotel in Cardiff. On the night of the event Mark picked me up from the station and whisked me up to our hotel room. Standing outside the room he instructed me to close my eyes and wait. The door opened a few minutes later. I was greeted by the sound of our special song. Mark then led me into the bedroom and told me to open my eyes. I looked down to see him kneeling before me. 'Will you marry me?' he asked. 'Yes', I replied without hesitation. He gently slipped the ring on to my finger and gave me a passionate kiss. The whole evening was magical.

We couldn't wait to get married and start our new life together and set a date for the following September. We had nine months to organise the wedding. My parents were shocked when we told them. Mum admitted she was very surprised because Mark wasn't my 'usual type', as she put it. 'And look what happened to all of those!' I replied. In the past, I had been led by my fearful ego in my search for love. It had encouraged me to focus externally and had decided what my 'type' was. In recent times, I had allowed my true self to lead me the way to love. Unlike my fear-based ego, my spirit had not let me down. It had taken me to true love, internally and now externally.

The healing power of a true love relationship

However, true love with The One does not mean living in a fantasy world without any challenges. It is not all 'sweetness and light'; as we discovered for ourselves, we cannot experience the light if we do not have the darkness too. As the wedding drew closer, certain issues surfaced. Mark and I both went through some extremely painful experiences involving our respective families. In addition, we had to deal with our ego-based fears, some unprocessed emotional baggage from the past, and numerous other personal issues, some of which we triggered in each other. I was finding it very challenging, particularly as I was simultaneously finishing my degree, doing the NLP diploma and starting to organise the wedding!

But, throughout that time, even in the darkest moments, my love for Mark never altered. I frequently reminded myself of the vision and feelings I had had that day in the supermarket. I remembered the person I fell in love with, the one he truly is underneath the personality and the ego. Each time we came up against an issue I became more able to step back from the drama and see the truth in the situations, as did Mark. Remembering not to play the role of victim, blaming Mark, members of my family, or other people or situations for my pain, and instead working at healing the emotional buttons that were pressed in me also helped. Mark worked through his issues too. In addition, during that time I learnt that having a true love relationship with myself also needed continuous commitment and effort.

Marrying The One

As I walked up the aisle on our wedding day, towards the amazing man standing waiting for me, I felt the tears welling up inside me. After everything I had experienced in my life, the self-loathing, the heartache, the loneliness, the M.E., the lifestyle changes and many dark nights of the soul, I was about to marry The One for me.

To some of the guests in the church it probably seemed to happen very suddenly and may have looked like a whirl-wind romance. It might have even seemed like a miracle that I was walking up the aisle at all that day, with all the male encounters and relationship challenges I had experienced.

Nevertheless, I knew the truth. I had made it happen, with the support of the Universe. I had been brave enough to turn within. I had committed to knowing myself, loving myself, changing my thoughts, healing my emotions, teaching others how to treat me, nurturing my true self and making time for my passions and childlike fun. I had uncovered what I wanted, had asked for it, had focused on becoming The One myself first and had let go. I had radically improved the relationship with myself and had discovered true love. This alone made it all worthwhile.

However, I also knew what it had taken me to reach the point of recognising true love in someone else when it walked into my life. Mark was the icing on my gluten-free wedding cake!

PART TWO

The Seven Secrets
on
How to Find True Love

Introduction

What is true love?

Prior to embarking on the less conventional route of searching for true love within myself first as part of my healing, I believed that true love was painful. I thought the deeper the heartache, the more I must be in love with the person: after all, 'love hurts' as the saying goes. The cinematic version of true love supports this, probably because it is dramatic and makes for better entertainment. In addition, the filmmakers seem to want us to believe that despite all the drama and conflict, the protagonists often live 'happily ever after'.

However, thanks to the lessons I learnt during my own search for true love as described in Part One, I now perceive this as pseudo love or co-dependency, which may or may not result in happiness in the short term, but ultimately leads us towards unhappiness in the long term. When we perceive ourselves as, or feel that we are, dependent on another person to receive love, to be or feel lovable, we are confusing true love with co-dependency.

Furthermore, true love doesn't hurt. In my experience, what hurts is when the other person triggers something in us, an emotional wound that has not been dealt with and healed (unless, of course, it involves abuse, which is another matter – but it is still not love). I also learnt that pain and unhappiness arise when we deny, repress or ignore our own needs and when we look to another person, activity or substance to make us happy. When we acknowledge and fulfil our own needs and make ourselves happy, we begin to liberate ourselves from co-dependency and discover true love instead.

A simple checklist to help you recognise true love

In the past, because I did not know what true love looked like, I spent many unhappy and confusing years with The Others in my search for true love and The One, as my story demonstrates. I eventually learnt that there are some clear differences between a co-dependent relationship and a true love relationship. I include a simple checklist (entitled 'How to Distinguish The One from The Other') of these differences at the end of this introduction in the hope that, whether you are single or in a relationship, it helps you to recognise and clarify what true love means for you.

The qualities in the checklist describing The One also illustrate some of the key ingredients of developing a healthy, loving relationship with yourself. A true love relationship with The One, for example, does not feel like work. The work is changing the relationship with yourself so that rather than being dependent on another to meet your needs, or for love, you find what you are seeking by developing this type of relationship with yourself.

If you are in a relationship, some of the qualities of The Other may apply equally to you as to your partner. You may, for example, be convincing yourself that your partner could be The One but you are seeing other people behind their back, as I did in some of my relationships. This reflects a search for an external solution to meeting your needs rather than fulfilling them yourself, which fuels dependency.

The seven secrets

According to Co-dependents Anonymous UK, the cause of co-dependency is 'long-standing destructive patterns of living'. They divide these patterns into four categories: 'denial', 'low self-esteem', 'compliance' and 'control'. You will notice as you work through the Seven Secrets, finding out who you are and learning to be true to yourself, that these are all addressed. Thus you will find that you will begin to free yourself from the patterns of co-dependency, discovering the true love that lies within you and the opportunity for happiness in the long term.

In addition, it is my hope that, if you are unclear at the moment what true love looks like, as you work through the Seven Secrets and use the simple checklist, you will be able to formulate and clarify your own personal belief about what is true love, learn to distinguish The Other from The One and find the true love that was within you all the time.

In order to facilitate the process of working through the Seven Secrets, I recommend first reading through each of them, going at your own comfortable pace, to the end of this section of the book. Then, when you are willing, begin the exercises, again doing whatever you can in the time you can allocate to yourself. Although I have described these as 'Secrets' instead of steps, because they are based on timeless universal laws which can be approached in any order and are interconnected, there is a natural sequence to them. Secrets One and Two form the foundation layer of developing the healthy, nurturing and loving relationship with ourselves that we seek with another. Secrets Three and Four further enhance this. The emphasis shifts slightly for the last three Secrets to how we can benefit from the all-encompassing Universe in terms of finding true love and The One.

As you read through these Secrets, you might find you have some resistance to changing. You might have the belief that you do not have enough time to do what is required. However the resistance might arise, allow yourself to be aware of it and relax, knowing that it is a very natural part of the process. Be kind to yourself and be prepared to adjust your habits accordingly to make the time for yourself, even if it might mean watching less television, or getting up a little earlier on some days. Remind yourself of what made you pick up this book in the first place and what you want in your life. In my experience it is always possible to make time for ourselves and overcome any resistance we might have, if we are willing, want something enough and persevere.

Although only you can do what is necessary to change and find the true love and happiness that you are seeking, I invite you to seek support whenever you feel you need it, whether it's from a trusted friend or relative, a therapist or coach, or even celestial support such as asking the angels for help. Allow yourself to experiment with it and do whatever you find works for you.

It's also important to be your own supporter and champion of change, to keep you motivated on your journey. Therefore, I also encourage you to congratulate and validate yourself every step of the way as you progress along your path to finding true love, starting with the fact that you have bought and are reading this book.

How to Distinguish
'The One' from 'The Other'

The One	The Other
Is loving	Is unloving, possibly even abusive (psychologically, physically etc.)
Takes responsibility for themselves	Plays the role of victim or bully
Makes observations when asked	Judges and criticises you
Is patient and understanding	Is impatient and intolerant
Is respectful of you and your beliefs	Is disrespectful of you and/or your beliefs
Is honest	Is not completely honest
Is open	Is closed
Is trustworthy	Is untrustworthy
Is faithful	Is unfaithful
Makes time for you and the relationship	Doesn't make time for you or the relationship
Openly communicates	Manipulates (overtly or covertly by withholding emotionally, sexually, etc.)
Respects your boundaries	Pushes your boundaries
Doesn't try to control you	Tries to control or dominate

The One (cont'd)	The Other (cont'd)
Makes requests	Makes demands
Is secure	Is jealous and needy
Is intimate	Is distant and aloof
Meets their own needs	Depends on you to meet their needs
Balances their own needs with the needs of others	Plays The Martyr
Accepts you for who you are	Tries to change you
Encourages you to be all you can be	Tries to hold you back and keep you small
Understands that only you can make yourself happy	Believes they can make you happy and says no-one will love you as they do
Enjoys being with you but is also able to be alone	Believes (or says) they can't live without you
Is supportive	Is unsupportive
This relationship thrives on harmony	This relationship thrives on drama
This relationship feels effortless	This relationship feels like hard work

SECRET ONE

Know yourself

Life in the 'asleep zone'

How well do you really know yourself? How aware of your thoughts are you? Do you know how often you think negatively about yourself? Are you aware of the words you use to describe yourself? Would you say you were very much in touch with your feelings? Do you know what motivates you to behave the way you do, particularly regarding love and relationships? Do you know who you are at your deepest core, beyond the roles that you play and the person you portray to others?

These are questions that not many of us spend time consciously thinking about. We do not often consciously observe the thoughts we think, the words we speak, the sensations in our body or our true feelings. In contrast, we frequently live in a trance-like state, operating on automatic pilot, living in what I call the 'asleep zone'. We repeatedly treat ourselves like robots, pushing ourselves too hard, keeping constantly busy and neglecting our fundamental needs such as getting sufficient rest and regular exercise, let alone attending to our innermost desires.

Living life in this way has a negative impact on us, whether we are aware of it or not. When we do not know ourselves well enough, we commonly look outside of ourselves for a solution to our malaise and for the love that we feel is missing in our lives. This and the other unconscious behaviours mentioned become our habits, shaping and dictating our lives. We are, in effect, asleep to ourselves as we go through life. And we might wonder why we're not happier!

Until we embark on an inner journey, we have what could be referred to as a surface level of self-awareness. We know what food we like and what we dislike. We might be aware that we enjoy dancing but hate going to the gym. In terms of a partner, we might be consciously aware that we prefer muscular people to thin people, or tall people to short people.

Although these preferences have an impact on our search for true love, their influence is minor compared to that of the deeper, hidden aspects of ourselves such as our level of self-esteem, our unhealed emotional wounds and our fears. These reside in our unconscious mind, out of our conscious awareness, until we choose otherwise.

The reason we may resort to using defence mechanisms such as repression and denial to keep these aspects hidden from our conscious awareness is usually because we are afraid to face our fears, our wounds and other issues. We might bury our head in the sand, blame others, bad luck or circumstances, become stuck in indecision, or constantly go from one romantic or sexual encounter to the next. Similarly, we might repress our real feelings, attempting to keep them out of our awareness with alcohol, drugs, food, shopping, sex or excessive busyness. Focusing externally, on other people, substances or activities, is a way we maintain the patterns of denial and repression.

We also commonly use these defence mechanisms because on some level we believe it helps us to suffer less than if we were to face ourselves and our pain. We often do it because we are unaware of the power of the unconscious mind, and of what is hidden from our awareness, to determine our success in terms of true love and happiness. We are unable to change that which we are consciously unaware of and so until we take action to increase our self-awareness, the unconscious mind is able to exert its power over us. Consequently, it causes us to react to others in ways we would rather not, to attract unsuitable partners and to become dependent on others to fulfil our needs: in other words, to become co-dependent.

A specific example of the power the unconscious mind has on our search for true love is of being convinced on a conscious level that we are ready for a committed relationship but finding ourselves continually attracted to partners who are not in a position to commit, either emotionally or physically. If we dig deeper, we may become aware that we are attracting these people to us because in fact we have a fear of intimacy ourselves.

We might have a fear of being alone and/or being left on the shelf, which we try and repress by going from one relationship to the next. Similarly, we may have an unconscious fear of rejection which leads us to reject others before they can reject us.

Even if we are in a discontented relationship, we may still harbour a fear that our partner will leave us and so we may put our partner's needs first and deny our own, in the hope that they will remain in the relationship. We may also do our utmost to evade conflict in an attempt to avoid upsetting our partner and, again, repress our needs in order to achieve this goal.

We sometimes perceive ourselves as being stuck, unsure which choice to make about our relationship: whether to remain in it or to leave. This confusion helps us to avoid our truth, as deep down we usually know what we need to do but are too afraid to do it. Instead we repress it, keeping it out of our conscious awareness under the guise of confusion or indecisiveness.

In reality, if we allow ourselves to continue the patterns of denial and repression we perpetuate our suffering. We will continue to find ourselves alone and unhappy, or in a discontented relationship, dependent on external sources for our happiness and, ultimately, trapped and powerless, as my story demonstrates.

We often have a tendency to prefer what we perceive as the security of the known, even when it means continuing to be discontented. However, shifting our focus towards our inner life and increasing our self-awareness is necessary if we want to liberate ourselves from suffering, from a co-dependent life with The Other, and find real happiness. John Bradshaw demonstrates this in his book *Home Coming*: 'It is impossible to be intimate if you have no sense of self. How can you share yourself with another if you do not really know who you are? How can anyone know you if you do not know who you really are?' (p.18).

Benefits of knowing yourself

Empowers you to create the life and love you desire

When we do not know ourselves beyond the surface layer, we are usually unaware of our unconscious self-sabotaging patterns, our fears and so on. Consequently, we find ourselves thinking, feeling and behaving in the same way that we have always done. All we can do when we are not consciously aware of ourselves is address the symptoms of our unhappiness. In this way, the past will continue to have a hold over us and we will experience more suffering on our own or discontentment in our relationships.

Thus, one of the key benefits of increasing our level of self-awareness, by letting go of the patterns of denial and repression and becoming consciously aware of our self-sabotaging patterns, is that we empower ourselves to address the root causes of our unhappiness. With this knowledge, we can access the truth of what is going on in our lives and we are then in a position to break free from the past and create the life and love we desire. We liberate ourselves to *act* rather than *react*. We discover who we really are, what we really need, in mind, body and spirit. Only when we know what our needs are, what makes us happy, can we give this to ourselves.

Become more self-reliant

Like many people, when I was unhappily single I sought love and happiness outside of myself. The possibility that I could make *myself* happy did not enter my conscious awareness. Similarly, during my discontented relationships, I spent time trying to figure out if the guy I was with was The One or not and whether I should stay in the relationship or end it. I asked friends for their opinions and advice on what to do, and later I turned to a psychic for quick answers rather than taking the time to discover – or trust – the answers within myself.

Although friends, psychics, therapists and other professionals can be very helpful and are often able to give us incredibly useful guidance and support, the only person that knows the answers for you, the 'right' choice for you to make, is *you*. In addition, the only person that can make you happy is *you*. We all have the ability to rely on ourselves for our own happiness because the love we seek is within us (see Secret Two), which begins with consciously knowing ourselves. Therefore, by improving our level of self-awareness, we can become more self-reliant and thus more self-empowered in the process.

Harness your inner strength

Getting to know ourselves beyond the surface level enables us to wake up to our spirit, also referred to as our true self, as introduced in Chapter Nine. It is the part of us that exists even when our relationship, our job, our health or our wealth have been stripped away. The benefit of waking up to our spirit is that we learn to recognise that it is who we really are. It is a source of great inner strength and as such it can support us in dealing with life's challenges, especially love and relationship issues. Furthermore, our spirit helps us not only to deal with, but also to triumph over, adversity. It inspires us to challenge our 'fate' and instead take control of our own destiny. Therefore, whether it's a long, unhappy period without a relationship, a relationship full of conflict, a divorce or another issue, by becoming consciously aware of and connecting with this powerful aspect of ourselves, we can harness our inner strength and turn our lives around.

How to know yourself

Getting to know ourselves on a deeper level requires action. It also involves becoming a seeker of the truth, rather than seeing what we want to see. We need to be honest with ourselves, and prepared to discover both the pleasant aspects of ourselves such as our strengths and our dreams, but also the more challenging parts such as our fears, our emotional wounds and any negative self-perceptions. We need to let go of the habit of repressing the challenging aspects through alcohol and drugs and, instead, allow them to come into our conscious awareness. As with any relationship, it takes time to get to know ourselves deeply. The purpose of this section is to help you get started.

Make time for reflection and self-enquiry

The process of reflection and self-enquiry is an easy one for you to begin with. It takes around 20 minutes. However, once you become familiar with the process, you can do it anywhere, any time and for the amount of time you want – even taking five minutes in the toilet during work can help!

Exercise

Turn the phones off and take any other measure you can to ensure you are not disturbed. Take a notepad and pen, sit in a comfortable chair and prepare to begin.

Once you are ready, take a few moments to notice exactly what you are experiencing in this moment. How do you see yourself as a person? What sort of things are you saying to yourself? How does your body feel? How do you feel emotionally? Or are you perhaps numb to your feelings? Are your thoughts focused on the exercise or are they drifting off onto something else instead? Just allow yourself to become aware of what you are experiencing for a few moments.

Now, take a few deep breaths and allow yourself to focus on an issue that is currently bothering you – perhaps your current relationship status or relationship challenge. As you focus your mind on this issue for a moment, write down any thoughts that come to you regarding it, using the format 'I think . . . x, y, z . . . about it/him/her'.

As you contemplate your issue, observe how your body feels now. What sensations can you feel? Do you feel more relaxed or not? What are you feeling emotionally right now?

Has how you perceive yourself changed at all? What are you saying to yourself as you contemplate your issue? How do you feel about yourself and the issue and the other person (if there is someone else involved) now? Ask yourself what buttons this person pushes in you. What emotions do they trigger?

As you become more consciously aware of your thoughts, perceptions, feelings, emotions and so on, take a moment to write them down in your notepad. When you have finished writing, take some time to reflect on what you have written. Notice what you consciously know about yourself in relation to your issue and the effect it is having on you. This information will assist you on your journey, even if you can't quite see how yet. Give yourself a pat on the back for taking a significant step forward towards experiencing true love and happiness in your life.

Observe your internal self-talk and external language

As previously explained, our unconscious mind is very powerful, but it has no sense of humour; hence, everything is all 'truth' to the unconscious mind. For example, although on a conscious level we may jokingly put ourselves down in front of others, our unconscious mind takes what we have said as a true statement. This filters through to our psyche and in turn affects the way we feel about ourselves. In addition, it affects how others treat us and so if we put ourselves down all the time, others will do likewise.

Therefore, you need to become consciously aware of the language you use about yourself, which includes your internal 'self-talk' and the way you talk to others about yourself.

Exercise: *Liver* moments

My own way of making the process of changing the way we talk about ourselves easier and more fun is using what I call '*Liver* moments'. You need to enlist the support of a trustworthy friend or relative, therapist if you have one, or anyone who's positively supportive of your personal development. Next, choose a certain food or drink or similar item that you hate. I happen to hate liver.

When you have thought of the item, label this your '*Liver* Moment'. Then ask your confidant to tell you, using *your* label, when they hear or notice you putting yourself down, sharing limiting beliefs such as 'I'm not capable of doing that', or berating yourself by saying such things as 'I shouldn't have done that'. When your support person catches you talking about yourself in this way, they need to bring this to your attention by saying 'That's a (*insert your chosen item*) Moment!'

In the beginning it is useful to notice how many '*Liver* Moments' you spot yourself, and how many your support person points out to you. Then, notice any patterns such as certain people, places or situations that trigger this negative or limiting self-talk in you.

As your self-awareness increases and you can see clearly which people, places or situations trigger a negative response in you, in addition to healing your emotional wounds that are triggered, you need to switch focus. It is time to observe how many *positive*, affirming statements you use about yourself in a day – ask your support person to join you in this. Notice the patterns that you have changed, the people, places and situations that no longer trigger you to react negatively, and congratulate yourself for the change you have created in your life.

Observe, sense and listen to your body

In order to enhance your self-awareness, it is also important to become consciously aware of what we think about our bodies, how we perceive them, how we feel about them and how we treat them.

Exercise

Take a few moments to allow yourself to focus on your body, noticing the thoughts and feelings you have about your physical self, and record them in your notepad. Ask yourself which parts of your body you love and what aspects you dislike, or even hate. How do you treat your body? What condition are you in? What does your body need in order to feel genuinely energised throughout the day? Do you drink alcohol, smoke or take drugs? If so, be honest with yourself about the quantities you consume and notice what motivates you to do so. Do you find it easy to relax? What do you need to help you relax? Does this support your personal growth? What are your stress levels? What stress-relieving, or prevention, methods do you use, if any? How often do you exercise? What do you need in order for you to commit to regular exercise? How willing are you to commit to changing your habits where necessary and giving your body what it really needs, both physically and nutritionally?

Reflect on the notes you have made. Notice what these insights may tell you about your relationship with your physical self and how much you are or are not meeting your real needs. This information will help with Secret Two in particular.

Open up to your spirit

In addition to knowing our mind and body, we need to get to know our spirit or true self. In order to do this, it helps to be honest with yourself about your current beliefs concerning this concept.

Exercise: Part one

Take a few deep breaths before you begin. Now, ask yourself whether or not you currently believe you have a spirit or a true self. Do you believe there is a part of you that is full of love, inner peace, joy and wisdom, even if you do not seem to be consciously connected to it at the moment? As you reflect on the concept of your spirit, make a note of the thoughts, images, sounds or feelings that come to you about it. If this appears a little strange, ask yourself how willing you are to challenge, or suspend, this belief in order to help you find true love.

We can become consciously aware of our spirit only when we are relaxed and grounded in our body. Thus, when you decide you are ready to begin to consciously connect with this aspect of yourself, you will find it easier if you relax. Many people find it easier to relax if they avoid consuming tea, coffee, chocolate or anything else containing caffeine prior to beginning their conscious connection time. Therefore, you may find it helpful to do the next exercise first thing in the morning, particularly before your mind becomes too busy.

Exercise: Part two

This is a deep, conscious breathing exercise. You may like to begin doing it for five minutes for the first few days, working up to a period of 10 minutes, or longer if you like, as you progress on your journey.

Ensure your phones are turned off. Now find a comfortable place to sit. Ideally, have your back straight and your legs crossed or, if you prefer to sit in a chair, sit with your legs uncrossed and both feet on the ground. Place your hands gently in your lap. You can close your eyes or leave them open, whichever is more comfortable for you and enables you to stay awake!

Now, take a moment to breathe in deeply and slowly through your nose and out through your mouth. After a few deep breaths, allow yourself to observe your breath as you inhale and exhale. Feel the coldness of the air as you breathe in and the warmth of the air as you breathe out. As you continue to breathe in through your nose and out through your mouth slowly, deeply and calmly, allow any thoughts you might have to float through your mind, like clouds in the sky. Simply allow them to be what they are and continue focusing on your breath. You may find your mind wandering off: just notice it and bring your attention back to focusing on your breath as you inhale and exhale. Continue the deep, conscious breathing until you have reached the time you set aside for yourself.

Other practices that assist the process of consciously connecting to your spirit include meditating (see Further Reading), walking in nature and Tai Chi. More are mentioned throughout Part Two of the book. Whatever practice you choose, it is important to commit to doing it regularly and at the same time every day, as far as is practically possible. This helps the practice to become a natural habit, just like brushing your teeth, rather than something you have to remember to do.

Take up yoga

Yoga has gained in popularity in recent years, possibly because it has been marketed as a way to keep fit and lose weight. However, yoga is one of the best practices for increasing the conscious awareness of your mind, body and spirit, especially the slower, more reflective forms which include some meditation. (See Other Resources for more on yoga.)

Attend workshops

Workshops are a great place to get to know yourself because new insights into your own patterns and personal challenges can be gained from hearing others share their experiences. It is also beneficial to experience the support of being with like-minded people who are interested in developing themselves, becoming happier and finding true love. (See Other Resources for further details.)

Experience one-to-one psychotherapy, coaching, NLP or counselling

One of the principal benefits of one-to-one professional help is greater conscious awareness of ourselves. It can prove especially beneficial in the early stages, as I found in my own personal journey, to have one-to-one sessions with someone in the helping profession. In order to decide what is best for you, I suggest contacting the relevant associations (see Other Resources), or a qualified therapist, coach, NLP practitioner or counsellor directly. You could also speak to people you might know who have benefited from professional help. They may be able to refer you to someone.

Go on a retreat

Retreats are another excellent way to increase your conscious awareness of your mind, body and particularly your spirit. There are numerous retreats of various durations, both in the UK and abroad (see Further Reading).

Journalling

In addition to recording what you discover about yourself, as recommended in the exercises in Part Two of this book, it is very useful to make a note of your thoughts, feelings, observations and insights on a daily basis, or whenever you feel you want to, in a private journal. It is a very therapeutic form of expression.

Read other books

In addition to the points included in this section, knowing yourself is a fundamental part of all the other Secrets; thus, as you work through them your knowledge of yourself will naturally increase. Furthermore, there are many other self-development books available which can assist you in increasing your level of self-awareness. Having said that, it is important to acknowledge, as I discovered myself, that reading on its own rarely creates change. It took me five years after reading my first self-help book to finally work through the exercises and consciously begin to know myself. It was a key part of transforming the relationship I had with myself and finding true love.

SECRET TWO

Love yourself

A challenging concept

We are generally conditioned to believe that love is something we can and should obtain from an external source, from someone outside of ourselves. It is socially acceptable to seek love in this way – in fact, it is expected. Hence we go from one relationship to another in pursuit of The One, or we stay in our discontented relationships and seek love in the arms of others. We may, albeit unconsciously, turn to food, alcohol, drugs, shopping or gambling in our desperate external search for love.

Investing time and energy in loving ourselves is not particularly common either, and it has negative connotations largely because of the perception that it is narcissistic. If, for example, we are asked to think of someone who loves themselves, we probably think of a person who has an over-inflated ego, is vain and spends a lot of time looking at themselves in the mirror. However, in reality this person has no real self-love, of their mind, body or spirit. Rather, their love is a false love, of an image. Sometimes we understand that loving ourselves is not about having an over-inflated ego, or being in love with the image of ourselves. Nevertheless, because we may harbour hidden feelings of negativity or less than loving thoughts about ourselves, we might continue to find the concept of self-love threatening, even frightening, and therefore judge it as wrong or selfish until we start to change.

Self-deprecation, on the other hand, is often perceived as an attractive quality. Our society encourages us to put ourselves down. We may believe it keeps us humble, enables other people to feel more comfortable in our presence and helps us to fit in. Hence, we often find it easier to admit to others our perceived negative qualities than our positive ones. At a personal development workshop, for example, when participants were asked to list three main positive *qualities*, the majority of those questioned automatically listed three *activities* they perceive as positive. They mentioned doing volunteer work, listening to others and taking care of a neighbour's child, rather than qualities they possess such as being caring, compassionate and generous.

Nevertheless, irrespective of how socially acceptable these behaviours or habits are, seeking love outside of ourselves first, putting ourselves down and denying or repressing our positive qualities lowers our self-esteem, our sense of self-worth, which in turn leads us to treat ourselves less than well and fosters co-dependency. In effect we are giving our power away to others. Although it may be unusual, even uncomfortable, to acknowledge our positive qualities to ourselves (or to others when asked to) and to cease the pattern of self-deprecation, it becomes easier the more we focus on improving the relationship we have with ourselves. Furthermore, this is essential if we are to find true love and happiness.

Other blocks to loving yourself

Our distaste for developing a loving relationship with ourselves may not only be due to our previous misconceptions about the concept or our desire (whether conscious or unconscious) to conform, a fear of being socially rejected, or just a lack of awareness of the harm that we were doing to ourselves with self-deprecation. We may also have learnt the mistaken belief that we are unlovable and that love does not exist within us. So what causes us to develop these erroneous beliefs about ourselves? The answer usually lies in painful childhood experiences.

During our childhood we may have received unloving messages, explicitly or implicitly, from our parents, siblings, other relatives, teachers or peers. These messages may have included 'I have no time for you', 'you are unimportant', 'you are helpless', 'you are a nuisance', 'you should be ashamed of yourself', 'you are ugly' or 'you are stupid', and numerous others. Receiving these messages would probably have led us to feel anything from abandoned, rejected, neglected and lonely to 'not good enough' and unworthy. This in turn reinforced the erroneous message that love is not within us and, as a result, we seek in someone or something else what we perceive we lack in ourselves.

Seeking love outside of ourselves at the expense of developing a loving relationship with ourselves blocks true love and leads to co-dependence. Other blocks include fearing that if we try to love ourselves we might not be able to, because of the messages we heard as children; continuing to blame other people for our unhappiness and the problems in our lives; holding on to anger and resentment; lack of forgiveness; wanting to seek revenge; or continuing to feel guilty or ashamed about something we did in the past. Similarly, repressing, denying or neglecting our mental, physical, emotional or other needs and treating our bodies with disrespect or abusing ourselves also acts as a block to true love.

Another way we sabotage our happiness is by believing that it is easier to focus on finding love externally rather than healing the relationship we have with ourselves. By putting our happiness and love in the hands of another, though, we dis-empower ourselves and impair our self-esteem. Consequently, we usually find we do not feel good about ourselves unless we are in a relationship, and so we become unhappily single. Similarly, when we do form a relationship, we become co-dependent on our partner for our love and happiness, which leads to a relationship with The Other rather than The One. We then find ourselves living in fear of our partner leaving and taking the love and happiness with them, as my story illustrates.

However, all the love that we need is within us, as Dr Doreen Virtue confirms in *Healing with the Angels*: 'love is already within each of us, and we don't need another person in our lives in order to feel loved' (p.22). Therefore, as demonstrated here and throughout this book, seeking love internally, by developing a healthy, nurturing and loving relationship with ourselves, is essential if we are to free ourselves from co-dependency and find true love.

Benefits of loving yourself

Improved relationships

It is a universal truth that the love we seek is already within us, and also that we are only able to love others to the extent to which we love ourselves. Therefore, loving yourself improves relationships. When we become more consciously aware, we realise that our happiness is our responsibility, not our partner's. We stop trying to achieve the impossible, to make our partner change because we want them to and because we think that is what the solution is. In developing a healthy, loving relationship with ourselves, we work to release our own blocks to true love and intimacy, we increase our self-esteem and sense of self-worth, and we become kinder and more compassionate towards ourselves and our partner and subsequently our relationship improves. Similarly, it improves our relationships with our relatives, friends and colleagues too, which is explained further in Secret Three.

Deeper trust

If we are in a relationship with The Other, we may find that our partner is unable to cope with the new nurturing and loving relationship we have with ourselves, for many reasons. The benefit of developing a loving relationship with yourself is that even if this happens, because our self-esteem and sense of self-worth increase when we give ourselves what we need, we are able to accept their decision. We are able to move on with our lives because we are no longer in fear, or dependent on our partner for our love. Being consciously aware that we have the power to create our own love and happiness creates a deeper trust in ourselves and, in turn, in the process of life.

Experience the power of forgiveness

Anger, bitterness, hatred and guilt are powerful emotions relating to unforgiveness. These emotions keep us stuck, depressed, unfulfilled and unhappily single or discontented in our relationships. Hence, even if we deny it or are not consciously aware of the fact, we continue to suffer long after the event, as demonstrated in my story.

We often want to be right and thus it is easier to continue to blame the other person for what we perceive they did to us, rather than confront and work through the anger and pain held within us. When we do this, though, we are punishing ourselves and depriving ourselves of happiness.

Therefore, we need to ask ourselves: do we want to be right or do we want to be happy?

In order to free ourselves from these chains of the past, we need to do whatever it takes to enable us to forgive the other person (or ourselves) and give ourselves the chance of true love and happiness, as Caroline Myss confirms in *Anatomy of the Spirit*: 'self-love means caring for ourselves enough to forgive people in our past so that the wounds can no longer damage us' (p.204).

Obviously we cannot change our childhoods or any painful events that may have occurred in the past. Neither can we turn back time and erase something that we did to someone else, or to ourselves. Nevertheless, we can change the way those experiences affect us today, set ourselves free from the pain of the past and reclaim our personal power through the act of forgiveness. Forgiving, however, does not mean forgetting and thus condoning our actions or the actions of others, as Colin Tipping in *Radical Forgiveness* points out: 'wise people forgive but do not forget' (p.58). In other words, we still need to maintain healthy boundaries with those that we have had issues with in the past, and remember that just because we have taken conscious action to change and release unforgiveness, the other person will probably not have.

How to love yourself

We can choose to put the relationship we have with ourselves first in the knowledge that loving yourself, as it is defined in this book, concerns developing the healthy, nurturing and loving relationship with yourself that you desire to have with another. It involves becoming aware of, revealing and consciously connecting with our true self, the part of us beyond our image, the part that remains when our roles, our job titles, our wealth have been stripped away. We don't need to shout about it or declare this to the world! It is best kept a private matter in order to protect your inner world, shared only with your therapist or trusted support person. This process begins with increasing our self-awareness even further.

Get to know yourself even better

If we are unhappily single or discontented in our relation-ship and desire true love, we need to honestly examine the relationship we have with ourselves. The more you con-sciously know yourself, not only your mental, emotional, physical and spiritual needs but also your fears, your values, how you feel about yourself, the easier it is to develop a loving relationship with yourself.

Exercise

Take a few moments now to examine the extent to which you love yourself currently. Your thoughts and feelings will assist you. You can start by asking if you like yourself and, if so, what qualities you have that you like. Then dig a little deeper by asking yourself if you think or sense that you're unable to be alone. Do you fear being left on the shelf or are you continuing to stay in a relationship which your intuition is telling you to leave? You can also review the simple checklist that follows the introduction to Part Two for guidance. Notice how much you are like The Other or The One in terms of how you treat yourself. How honest are you with yourself? Are you committed to meet-ing your own needs? Are you committed to meeting your own needs? How much do you encourage yourself to be all that you can be? What, if any, resistance or fears do you have about being more loving to yourself?

> Record your thoughts, feelings, insights and under-
> standings. Allow yourself to notice the insights you have
> obtained regarding how you perceive or feel
> about yourself.

Improve your thoughts and the language you use about yourself

Once you have an awareness of your current state of self-love, you can take steps to improve your thoughts and the language you use about yourself. To do this (as mentioned in Secret One), you need to uproot your negative thoughts and your limiting beliefs. In addition, you need to stop any harsh judgements and negative, self-deprecating language you use about yourself, both internally and externally, by becoming vigilant about the way you think and talk about yourself, noticing when you are being negative and choosing to break these habits. In addition to '*Liver* Moments' (mentioned in the previous chapter), NLP can further assist this process. Reading books on how thoughts and language affect the way we perceive ourselves and feel about ourselves (see Further Reading) can also be useful.

Forgive yourself and others

Blame, resentment, anger and frustration block forgiveness and therefore love. If you consider yourself to be a calm, harmonious person who doesn't get angry, but find yourself feeling frequently frustrated with aspects of your life such as a lack of money, job satisfaction, time or love in your life (as I used to), then you will be holding anger or some other harmful emotion within yourself, albeit at an unconscious level. Therefore, if you are willing to be honest with yourself about these feelings, take responsibility for them and do what is necessary to release them, you are half-way there.

Exercise to forgive another

Make a list of the people you know you blame or are angry or frustrated with, and the reasons why. Then, take the person or action from the top of your list and write a letter (*which is for your eyes only*) to the person. Vent your thoughts and feelings without censoring them in any way. Tell the person in your letter what you think and how you feel about them and what they did. If you have enough privacy, read the letter aloud to yourself. When you think or sense that you have said everything you want to say, dispose of the letter completely in any way you deem appropriate (shred it, burn it safely, etc.). Take a few moments to notice your thoughts and feelings about the person and the situation now. Allow some time before you complete the next step in order to honour your experience.

When you think or sense that you have let go of the blame, frustration and anger regarding this person, write another letter to the same person (also for your eyes only) but this time write from a place of kindness and compassion. This will usually come naturally to you when you have released the blame and anger. Write what you appreciate about them and what you have learnt from the experience. Again, if you deem it is safe to do so, read the letter aloud to yourself. You can even say, if you believe it, that you have forgiven them for what they did, even though you may not forget it. Safely and completely dispose of this letter too.

Exercise to forgive yourself

Make a list of what you blame or are angry at yourself for and follow the same procedure as above, but include an apology to yourself when you are writing the second letter. Apologise to yourself for letting yourself down, and if someone else was affected by your actions, apologise in the letter to them too. In addition, tell yourself what you have learnt from the experience and make a promise to yourself that you will do whatever you need to make more loving choices in future.

If you are experiencing frustration in your life but are not consciously aware of any feelings of anger, or if you know you are unwilling to forgive yourself or others, perhaps because you fear the experience will be repeated, it may be advisable to seek professional support. (For other suggestions on these areas see Further Reading and Other Resources.) The Hoffman Process (a powerful week-long experience rather like a psychological and emotional detox) is particularly useful for this. I did the process in 2006, several years after where my story finishes in this book, but I have included it here as it was transformational for me, as it was for others I know who have done it, especially with regard to the process of forgiveness.

Take care of your body

What we think and feel about our body and the way we treat it also shows us our current level of self-love (as described in Secret One). To love yourself, it is essential to treat your body like a revered temple rather than a machine and give it the nutritious food and drink that it requires, at the times it requires them. It is also important to limit your intake of sugar and salt-laden products, fast food, fried food, alcohol and so on. Your body also requires a regular, healthy and balanced amount of exercise, which also assists in the process of loving yourself.

Exercise

Using the knowledge about your physical self that you discovered doing Secret One, commit to making any changes that you know you need to make in order to be more loving towards yourself. This may include improving your diet, seeking the advice of a nutritionist (see Other Resources), giving yourself proper relaxation time, and experimenting with different forms of exercise (but check with your GP first if you have a medical condition) until you find something that you enjoy doing.

In addition, make a commitment to give yourself a nurturing treatment once a week, such as a massage, reflexology, or just a warm bath surrounded by candles and soft music. It is important to give yourself a foot or shoulder rub (and/or any other areas you can comfortably reach!), even if you pay for professional treatments, as it is a way of connecting with yourself and nurturing your body.

Balance work, rest and play

Doing anything to the extreme, excessively, is not a sign of self-love. Therefore, to love yourself, particularly your spirit, you need to have a healthy balance of work, rest and play in your life.

Exercise

Reflect on the amount of time you spend working, resting and playing. Give yourself a rough percentage of time for each, out of your day. What do you notice about this? Which area needs some re-balancing? What would you need to change to re-balance it? How much are you prepared to do that in order to assist you to find true love?

What, if any, resistance or fears do you have about spending your time differently in order to be more loving to yourself?

Nurture your spirit

Becoming consciously aware of your true self is essential to loving yourself because it is the part of us that *is* love. The more we can discern the messages of our spirit by paying attention to our gut feelings, for example, as opposed to the fearful voice of our ego, the easier it is to love ourselves.

To nurture our spirit we need to change any behaviours that dishonour us, such as lying to ourselves (or others), putting ourselves (or others) down, neglecting our body, judging or criticising ourselves (or others) whether mentally or verbally, and gossiping. We need to develop habits that honour us such as being authentic, speaking positively about ourselves (or others), taking care of our physical needs, making observations and being kind towards ourselves and others. In addition, the more we practice being in present time rather than thinking about the past or the future, the more we connect with our spirit. When we choose to push through our fears and create the life we dream of, we nurture our true self.

Also ensure that you give yourself regular experiences that nurture your spirit such as meditating, giving yourself Reiki (see Other Resources), walking in nature, connecting with animals, volunteering, expressing your creativity, having childlike fun just for the sake of it, and doing whatever makes your heart sing (see Secret Four).

Accept yourself

The more you get to know yourself and discover the negative thoughts you've been having about yourself (and/or others) until you committed to changing, you may be tempted to berate yourself further. It is therefore particularly important to accept both yourself and where you are on your journey, and treat yourself as you would an innocent child who is just learning to walk. Be kind and gentle with yourself and praise yourself for the steps you are taking as you face your fears and confront yourself.

Finally, our minds, bodies and spirits are connected. Thus, when we nurture our mind, for example by thinking more loving thoughts, our body and our spirit also benefit, and vice versa.

SECRET THREE

Be true to yourself

Are you being true to yourself?

If you're single, how often do you accept dates from people who you're not attracted to or don't really enjoy being with, in order to avoid being on your own? Do you sleep with people when they haven't actually asked you out, secretly hoping that it will lead to a relationship? How often do you repress and ignore your true feelings, your needs, your values and your boundaries, in your personal life or your work, in order to appease someone else, to avoid conflict, out of fear of saying 'no', or for any other reason?

If you're in a relationship, how often do you repress and ignore your true feelings, needs, values and boundaries in your personal life or your work? How frequently do you mask your true feelings because you fear it would cause your partner to end the relationship, leaving you alone? Do you ever withhold the truth from them because you fear you'll hurt them? How often are you submissive in the relationship, accommodating your partner's needs, requests and wishes and repressing your own? Do you ever tell yourself that your partner is the cause of your relationship problems and that they need to change so that you can experience true love? Or do you believe that finding a different partner is the answer?

What we do when we are not being true to ourselves

Whether we are single or in a relationship, it is common for us to go about our daily lives denying or repressing our true feelings and needs (as introduced in Secret One) rather than being true to ourselves. We often avoid facing our pain and healing our emotional wounds, choosing instead to mask them with alcohol or medication, for example. Similarly, we frequently wear a mask of pretence rather than reveal our true feelings to others.

We may find ourselves putting other people's needs before our own. We become overly accommodating, giving in to their demands, such as not doing something we would like to do because the other person does not want us to do it. We conform, doing what they want and what is expected of us. And it seems as though we never get to do what *we* want to do.

We are often overly concerned about what others think of us and what we do. We find it hard to say 'no', fearing it might result in conflict, hurt someone's feelings or cause them to withdraw their love or friendship from us. Rather than speak our truth, simply saying 'no' and making it clear that we do not want to do what they are requesting of us, we may make excuses instead, telling little white lies.

Another example of not being true to ourselves is being unfaithful, even if it is only emotionally, choosing to stay in a relationship with someone who does not love us as we want to be loved. We convince ourselves that what our partner doesn't know cannot hurt them, but it hurts us. The 'secrets', or withholdings, weigh heavy on our spirits and create a block to intimacy and true love. Equally, when we don't make our hearts sing (see Secret Four), for example staying in a job that we hate without making time to learn the skills we need in order to achieve our dream job, or not making time to do volunteer work for a cause we are passionate about, we are not being true to ourselves.

If we do not create space in our lives and commit to knowing ourselves, loving ourselves, making our hearts sing or deciding what we want and so forth, we are not being true to ourselves. Instead, we become a victim. As a result, we actually create more suffering and unhappiness for ourselves, as Dr Wayne Dyer explains in *Pulling Your Own Strings*: 'They [victims] find themselves doing things they really would rather not do or being manipulated into activities loaded with unnecessary personal sacrifice that breeds hidden resentment' (p.4).

In other words, when we become a victim, we inadvertently allow others to control us and our lives, thus rendering ourselves powerless to create the life we desire. The resentment that this breeds in us results in more anger and frustration for ourselves. Sometimes, on an unconscious level, we fight against our hidden feelings of powerlessness by trying to control the people and events around us. This takes us further away from true love and happiness.

Physical effects of not being true to ourselves

In addition to the psychological and emotional effects that we experience, being a victim rather than being true to ourselves can eat away at us and lead to illness. Our body tells us when we are not being true to ourselves if we pay attention to its signals. Sometimes, at an unconscious level, we become ill in order to avoid doing something someone wants us to do that we do not want to do. As mentioned previously, in doing so we avoid having to actually say 'no' to them. Being ill is a socially acceptable reason for getting out of doing something. In this way, we attempt to evade the risk of the person taking our action personally and upsetting them.

We may have a particular ailment that appears when we are with the people we feel unable to speak our truth to, whether it is our current partner, a relative, colleague, boss or friend. If the symptoms disappear when we are not in the presence of a certain person, but reappear when we are, it could be our intuition guiding us to be true to ourselves and honour our needs or our true feelings. Likewise, sometimes we notice the symptoms arise when we are doing the job our intuition is guiding us to leave, so we feel ill during the week, but well at weekends. The messages continue until we face the root cause of the issue. When we avoid facing the root causes of our issues they simply appear in other areas of our lives, although we may not make the connection unless we consciously reflect on how we really feel and what emotions are being triggered in us by other people or events.

As demonstrated in this chapter, living a life of denial and compliance rather than being true to ourselves impacts the relationship we have with ourselves and others, our well-being and our work. It dis-empowers us and lowers our self-respect, which in turn reduces our self-esteem and confines us to co-dependence. This subsequently leaves us trapped in a complicated life, full of drama, conflict, disharmony, possibly illness and debt. It also aligns us with the erroneous belief, discussed throughout this book, that love exists outside of us and thus it creates a block to true love. Speaking from experience, it takes a great deal of energy to live life from this draining, unfulfilling, dis-empowered, inauthentic and unhappy place.

Because this sounds such an unpleasant way to live, we may wonder why we do it. One of the reasons we allow ourselves to live this way is our numerous conscious and unconscious fears. These can include, to name but a few: fear of taking responsibility for our lives; fear of change; fear of the unknown; fear of upsetting the 'status quo'; fear of rejection; fear of ending up alone or fear that those we believe love us will withdraw their love or friendship if we don't do what they ask of us. Another reason is a lack of awareness. Unless we are on an inner journey, we are frequently unaware that we play the role of victim, give our power away to others, and of the harm that this causes us. We may think we are saving ourselves from unhappiness and conflict, when in the long term we are increasing our suffering.

Thankfully, as with the other Secrets, as our conscious awareness increases, we are able to make a different choice. Although knowing ourselves better can help us to improve the relationship we have with ourselves and others, it is only by following it up with action, of which being true to yourself is a fundamental part, that we achieve change and thus free ourselves from co-dependence and find the true love we desire.

Benefits of being true to yourself

Increased self-empowerment

Denying or repressing our needs (as described here and in Secret One) and complying with the wishes of others helps maintain our patterns of fearful living, lack of self-love and low self-esteem. If we increase our self-awareness but do not take action to follow up on our new awareness, it affects us negatively.

In contrast, letting go of these patterns of behaviour, increasing our awareness of our real feelings, honouring them and meeting our needs instead increases our self-empowerment. Hence, we learn to live an authentic life, to say 'no' to what we do not want in our lives and 'yes' to more positive experiences. The more we honour our true feelings and stand up for ourselves in this way, the more our self-empowerment naturally increases and the more liberated we become.

Experience greater self-respect

Another benefit of being true to ourselves is that by becoming aware of all of our feelings and needs (mental, emotional, physical and spiritual), in addition to committing to honour them and meet these needs regularly, rather than being compliant as we were, we take back control of our lives. This increased self-empowerment in addition to the greater control we have over ourselves and what we create in our lives in turn leads to greater self-respect.

Engender greater respect from others

Although we may have yet to realise it, we teach potential partners, existing partners, relatives, friends, colleagues and so forth how to treat us. Subsequently, they walk all over us, manipulate us and/or control us only when we allow them to. When we take action to change this by establishing clear, firm boundaries for what we will and will not accept into our lives, and are honest with ourselves and others, we will, with practice, stop resorting to manipulation to try and get our needs met. Others are then less likely to manipulate us. If they attempt to, we no longer allow it.

Improved sense of well-being

When we live an inauthentic life in the 'asleep zone' we often neglect our body's messages, repress our intuitive gut feelings and act out of fear, as described previously. Negative thoughts, feelings and behaviours take a great deal of effort to repress or cope with. They are energy-draining and tension-inducing. This stressful state subsequently weakens our immune system and impairs our health. In contrast, being true to yourself involves no longer tolerating an inauthentic life and, instead, changing our thoughts and behaviours so that we honour our true feelings and needs. Hence, we reduce the stress in our lives which improves our sense of well-being and happiness too.

How to be true to yourself

Be honest with others

Being true to yourself, as with all the Secrets, requires honesty, firstly with ourselves and then with others. It includes being congruent in what we think and then say: that is, we say what we think. However, we only do this when we are sure we have a positive intention regarding the other person. In other words, being honest and authentic does not mean venting our anger at the person we are angry at, or saying cruel things about someone else with the deliberate intention to harm them.

We also need to be careful of whether we are judging someone, particularly if we are asked to give an opinion, such as what we think about what someone else is wearing. In this instance, how the other person feels in what they are wearing is more important than our sharing our opinion, which may be based on judgement. Sonia Choquette illustrates these points aptly in *Trust Your Vibes*: 'Opinions can isolate and assault, while genuine truth, even though it may be hard to hear, never attacks anyone – instead it fosters understanding and mutual respect' (p.59).

We are not responsible for the way other people choose to feel about what we say and do. By being true to ourselves we may inadvertently push their buttons and trigger an emotional reaction from them and they may take it personally. This usually happens because there is an unhealed emotional wound in them. This is their issue, not ours. Our responsibility is to ensure that what we say and do, we do with kind intentions, from a place of kindness and compassion. It is our responsibility to learn to control our emotions and release any anger and frustration in a safe, responsible way, with no-one else (except perhaps your therapist if you have one, or in some other appropriate therapeutic context) present! It is also our responsibility to deal with what the other person's reaction triggers in us, that is, to examine our stuff and leave them to theirs. Otherwise, we will block our own path to true love.

Exercise

Take a moment to think about the most significant issue in your life currently. Allow yourself to imagine you are able to be totally honest with yourself about your thoughts and feelings regarding this issue, perhaps for the first time in your life. Imagine you are only able to write the truth in your journal. Journal your thoughts and feelings about the issue. Then, write about the process of being honest with yourself. How easy was it to be honest with yourself? What do you now consciously know about yourself? What changes do you need to make in your life regarding the issue?

Believe in yourself

Being true to yourself involves believing in yourself. To do this, you need to value your own thoughts and opinions above those of other people. You need to honour your values, to do what you think or feel is right for you and supports your personal development. You need to do this even in the face of opposition from others, as long as you are not intentionally harming them, as mentioned previously.

Exercise

Allow yourself to imagine what your life would be like if you truly believed in yourself 100 per cent. What changes would you make to your current life? What dreams would you pursue with your strong self-belief? What else is different about your new life? Record your thoughts, understandings and feelings and reflect on what you now know about yourself. Which of these changes are you willing to commit to making first?

Setting boundaries: creating a personal code

Being true to yourself means not being emotionally invested in earning the approval and good opinion of others. Rather, we set clear boundaries, for which we need to create a personal code.

Exercise

To create your own personal code, firstly reflect on your past experiences. Allow yourself to notice where you perhaps gave your power away by going back on your promise to yourself, allowed people to take advantage of you or manipulate you to meet their needs, or allowed their opinion to matter more than your own and squash your dreams in the process. Acknowledge the situations where you put yourself at risk or wanted to say 'no' but didn't, and state your fears around what made you not say 'no'. Once you have finished, reflect back on the information.

Secondly, take the above information and write what you would have liked to have done instead, had you been fearless. Again, reflect on the information when you've finished.

Thirdly, using the information that you have gained from the previous exercises, in addition to what you have learnt from this book so far combined with your own intuitive guidance about what is being true to yourself, make a list of what you will and will not accept for yourself in your life from now on.

Part of devising the personal code also includes discerning those people who are supportive of your personal growth and your desire to find true love. This means knowing who you can trust, even if it is only one other person. This needs to be someone you can reach out to when you are feeling low or vulnerable, someone who, even if they are attracted to you, will wait until you are through the crisis before trying to sleep with you! Otherwise, you risk attracting The Other again.

An example in my own personal journey was when I realised that every time I became stressed, I reached for alcohol, usually on an empty stomach. This led to my losing control and putting myself in situations that affected me negatively. I admit I did 'drink and dial'! Hence, my personal code included, among other things, committing to eating something before I drank any alcohol and to regulating my alcohol intake. I also committed to contacting a female friend, or seeing a therapist, when I believed I needed emotional support, rather than reaching for the nearest man in my vulnerable or drunken state.

Just say 'no'

Living an authentic life includes being able to say 'no'. This is easier when we have a personal code and know what we do and do not want in our lives. When saying 'no', resist the urge to explain your reasons why. Rather, say it firmly, repeating it as many times as necessary until the other person gets the message. Be prepared to be labelled 'selfish'. If someone calls you selfish, know that they are just reacting to not being able to get you to do what they want you to do. They may not know how to handle it initially, but that is for them to deal with. Again, as long as your intention is to be true to yourself and support your journey, and you are being honest as opposed to purposefully cruel (which your thoughts, feelings or intuition will normally reveal), then allow yourself to relax and leave them to their tantrum.

Exercise

Over the next few weeks practise saying 'no' in order to strengthen your assertiveness muscles. For example, when someone offers you an item of food or drink that you don't really want or that is not conducive to your healthy life-style, give yourself permission to say 'no'. Notice the thoughts and feelings this evokes in you. You may like to practise this using role-play with a trusted friend or seek the help of a qualified therapist or NLP practitioner to make the process easier for yourself. Move through your fear and on to more challenging things, and continue to stick to your resolve using your personal code to help you.

Listen to your body

To be true to yourself you also need to listen to your body and give it what it really needs. This may involve anything from changing your thoughts and healing your emotions to modifying your behaviour.

Exercise

If you are experiencing ill health, aches and pains, or are uncomfortable with your weight, be open to what your body may be trying to tell you. Be honest with yourself and notice if there is anything in your life that you are trying to run away from, a situation you really want to leave, or feelings that you are trying to avoid experiencing, or if you are doing something that deep down you want to stop doing.

Notice when the symptoms first began. What was going on for you around that time? How did you feel before the experience compared to afterwards? If you find this challenging, as with all the other points in the Secrets, either talk to your supportive friend or relative, or seek professional help from someone who can assist you in the process of obtaining insights into the cause of your ill health. You must, of course, always seek the advice of your GP first if you are unwell, or have persistent symptoms, but it is possible to seek other support at the same time.

Consciously connect with your spirit

When you consciously connect with your spirit, for example by meditating, being compassionate towards yourself, appreciating the little things in life and by working on your passions, you are being true to yourself.

Exercise

Make a commitment to yourself to follow your intuition and take action to do whatever it is guiding you to do. Make time for your dreams and desires, and for having fun (see Secret Four for further information). Notice what makes your heart 'sink' and vow to stop doing it. From now on focus and commit to spending more time on the things that positively support you and with people that do the same, and less on things and with people that do not.

Finally, when I first started to formulate ideas for this book, a client of mine asked if she could read me a poem she had just written. I was moved to tears when I heard her words. For me, it sums up perfectly the meaning of this Secret, and is another wonderful example of serendipity at work.

Be True

My Body tells me – But why don't I listen?
My Heart knows – But my head pleads ignorance!
Why can't I trust the one who is true
And knows the difference between me and you

The hurt and the crying
The long silent dying
The tears and the pain – it's all the same
How we suffer – in order to play a game

Why not break the rules – and set yourself free
'No! – Stay small I say!' – It's far safer that way

Safer for who?
Not Me – Not You!
For no one will grow – And no one will know
There's more to life than putting on a show

Be true to yourself in all that you do
At the end of the day – it's all down to you

© Kirandeep Kaur Chodha 03.03.05

SECRET FOUR

Do what makes your heart sing

Does your heart sing?

How often do you feel lonely? How much are you consumed by the search for The One? Do you often wonder when, where and how you will meet them? How worried are you that you may never meet The One? When you date someone casually, how often do you ask yourself if they could be The One? Do you know what your passions are? How much time do you dedicate to your passions? Do you ever have any healthy, childlike fun? Do you avoid spending time on your passions or having childlike fun because of fear of others judging you?

If you are unhappy in your current relationship, you can ask yourself similar questions. How often do you feel lonely? How consumed are you by the question of whether to stay in the relationship or leave? Do you worry about leaving because you fear your partner could be The One after all, but just hasn't made it clear to you yet? Do you get frustrated thinking that if only they'd change their ways, then you could be happy and still be with them? Equally, do you know what you're passionate about? How much time do you spend on your passions? How much time do you make for childlike fun in your life and in your relationship? Could you be avoiding spending time on your passions or having childlike fun because you fear your partner would disapprove or judge you for it?

Whatever our relationship status, when we are unhappy or dissatisfied it is common for us to strive to keep ourselves busy, overly committing to projects and events both at work and in our private lives, and not make time to discover our passions or have any childlike fun. We carry out these behaviours, maintain these patterns of repression and denial, in our (usually unconscious) attempt to avoid facing ourselves and our issues, as discussed in Secret One. We also allow ourselves to do this when we choose to comply with the norm, with what our partners, friends, relatives and peers would have us do, rather than be true to ourselves, as illustrated in Secret Three. This constant repression, denial, compliance and external search for happiness creates anxiety and is very stressful. It also keeps our focus on the future, robbing us of the opportunity to experience happiness in the present moment. All this negative mental energy drains us and makes our heart sink, which fuels co-dependence and blocks true love.

In addition, making our heart sing is one of our fundamental needs. It is essential to our happiness. Often, though, we put the responsibility for our own happiness in the hands of others, believing that they have the power to make us happy. There are people who on some level will want to rescue others, by making it their goal to try and make another person happy, as mentioned in my own story. They believe it is possible to do this, and that they can give the other person what they need to make this happen. They often do not have a particularly nurturing, loving relationship with themselves. As a result, they need to feel needed and in control, which they achieve when they form a relationship with a person whom they perceive needs rescuing.

Ultimately, when we focus on fulfilling the needs of others, trying to achieve the impossible task of making someone else happy, we encourage them to be dependent on us and thus find ourselves forming a co-dependent relationship with The Other.

Sometimes we do not believe that we have the ability to make ourselves happy, especially if we are recovering from a relationship break-up or have experienced other personal trauma in our lives such as abuse, bereavement, serious illness or other challenging life circumstances. Similarly, we may find ourselves thinking that we don't deserve to, or shouldn't, make our heart sing and have fun. We may feel uncomfortable, possibly even guilty, allowing ourselves to have fun and experience joy when we have lost someone close to us, or when a good friend, relative or others around the world appear to be suffering.

The child within

Additionally, when we do not commit to making ourselves happy and doing what makes our heart sing, we neglect another significant aspect of ourselves that assists us on the path to true love and finding The One. It is the part of us that needs fun in our lives. This part is our childlike self, frequently referred to as our 'Inner Child' (introduced in Chapter Nine). It is an aspect of ourselves which we often aren't consciously aware of, or that we deny, repress and ignore, until we embark on an inner journey.

Even though we have become adults, this childlike aspect of ourselves continues to exist within us. It is the part of us that cries out for love, attention and fun when we are busy being 'grown up', earning money, acquiring more material objects and seeking love and happiness outside of ourselves. Our Inner Child is also the part of us that remembers all of our childhood experiences, not only the enjoyable ones but the painful ones too.

While it is important to give our jobs the attention they require, ensure we keep a roof over our heads and so on, it must not be to the detriment of our Inner Child, as it is a part of making our heart sing and is a necessity if we wish to be happy. The challenge is that consciously connecting with this aspect of ourselves can be an unfamiliar experience for us.

As adults we can find ourselves ignoring or repressing this part of ourselves by choosing activities which our fearful ego convinces us are fun and lead to happiness. Hence, we turn to food, alcohol, drugs, shopping or perhaps gambling in our search. These ego-driven activities may give us an instant high, but it is brief and is followed by a low because these activities are no substitute for true love and happiness. They lead to the desire for more as the ego's appetite is insatiable. It is never content with what we have given it. John Bradshaw explains it like this in *Home Coming*: 'without a healthy inner life, one is exiled to trying to find fulfilment on the outside. This is co-dependence and it is a symptom of a wounded Inner Child' (p.9).

Obviously we have to eat and shop. Nonetheless, when we turn to these and other activities out of an emotional need, that is in order to distract ourselves or numb out to our pain with the erroneous belief that it will make us happy, we end up suffering. We become trapped in a cycle, becoming addicted to the highs and constantly trying to avoid the inevitable lows. Additionally, spending time on ego-driven activities that do not make our heart truly sing and have a negative impact on us on some level leads us away from our spirit, from true love and happiness, towards being unhappily single or in a relationship with The Other.

It is no-one's responsibility but our own to make ourselves happy, for which making our heart sing is fundamental. We all deserve it. It is not only an aspect of self-love but it also helps others as we spread our joy when we are joyous. It is infectious. People can feel it, even if they are not aware of exactly what it is. Therefore, making our heart sing can help the world become a better, happier, more peaceful place.

Each person has the potential to do what makes their heart sing and experience true joy, no matter what their childhood experience, current situation or fears, because joy and passion come from within us. Making our heart sing is a quality of our true self, not our fearful self. It is a natural expression of love and is therefore a choice. It is our responsibility and we owe it to ourselves if we wish to find true love and The One.

Benefits of doing what makes our heart sing

Experience greater happiness

There is a certain quality that we experience within ourselves and in our life when we make our heart sing by discovering and spending time on our passions and consciously connecting with our Inner Child. This quality, which some might refer to as 'zest', makes us feel alive and energised. Thus, when our heart sings, we find we do not feel depressed, angry, bitter, ashamed, guilty, lonely, unloved or unlovable, nor are we consciously aware of any physical pain in that moment, no matter how briefly or long it lasts. By taking responsibility for our happiness and making our heart sing we empower ourselves. It is part of finding out who we really are and being true to that. These are factors that assist us in the process of liberation from co-dependence. Hence, when we make time for regular doses of childlike fun and feed our passions, we put the joy back into our lives and experience greater happiness.

Makes us more 'attractive'

Fulfilling our passions and having childlike fun helps us to feel happier, as mentioned above. When we feel happier, even if we are not consciously aware of it, we emanate what can be described as positive 'vibes'. We probably have an understanding of this concept of vibes if we think about what it's like for us to be around someone who is depressed or angry compared to someone who is joyful and happy. It is commonly known that positive, happy people attract other people to them much more easily than those who are sad or depressed. Therefore, the more we enjoy ourselves and make our heart sing, the more positive vibes we emanate, thus attracting more positive experiences to ourselves and enhancing our potential for meeting The One. This point is explored further in Secrets Five and Six.

Improves creativity and inspiration

We might have a belief that we are not creative. We might have been criticised at a young age for our creative work, whether it was making something by hand, writing stories or painting, by our parents, teachers, siblings or peers. As a result we may have closed ourselves off to our creativity on some level. However, creativity and inspiration are elements of making our heart sing, living a passionate life and connecting to our spirit. When we ignore or change our negative belief and instead allow ourselves to experiment with childlike fun and creative activities, all sorts of opportunities open up to us. We can experience 'aha!' moments, unexpected insights into what we need to do to solve our relationship issue or to find The One. In addition, because we have unleashed our creativity and allowed it to flow, our life can become an inspiration to us and to other people.

How to make your heart sing

Making our heart sing involves allowing ourselves to discover more aspects of ourselves which may have been hidden in our unconscious awareness, by no longer ignoring, denying or repressing our passions and our childlike self. Rather than rescuing others, we need to focus on rescuing and nurturing ourselves. We need to discover and familiarise ourselves with our Inner Child and our hidden dreams, in addition to committing to giving ourselves time to have fun and fulfil our passions. In order to do this, though, we first need to release any blocks we might have to making our heart sing.

Release any blocks

In order to do what makes our heart sing, we need to let go of any blame, guilt, unforgiveness or feelings of unworthiness that might be preventing us from allowing ourselves this opportunity for happiness.

Exercise

Using the notes you have been making throughout this section of the book, allow yourself some time now to discover what, if anything, might be blocking you from doing what makes your heart sing. As you contemplate making your heart sing, notice whether you have any resistance to it and, if so, what the resistance is about – perhaps fear, feeling unworthy, a belief that it would be selfish? What are your thoughts about it? What are you telling yourself? What feelings does this evoke in you? What are your fears, if any, about it? How willing are you to commit to doing what makes your heart sing? Ask yourself what you need to do or change to help you to be willing to acknowledge and give time to your Inner Child. Reflect, without judgement, on where you are on your journey in regards to this. Then allow yourself to do whatever you need to, by working through the Secrets, or using other methods (see Other Resources) to release any blocks, such as fear, around making your heart sing.

Give yourself permission to play

If as a child you were not allowed to play, were criticised for playing or discouraged from doing so for whatever reason, you may need to give yourself permission to play. This is particularly important if as an adult you have a job with a great deal of responsibility and/or are very ambitious.

Exercise

Your task is to give yourself permission to play and do something to make your heart sing at this time in your life. Take a moment to notice whether or not you might have any resistance to giving yourself permission to play, for example making excuses such as a lack of time to play. If so, ask yourself what that is about. What issue(s) might underlie this reluctance to grant yourself permission? The information you obtained about yourself in Secret Two concerning how much balance you have in your life in terms of work, rest and play can help you here.

Reflect on your thoughts, beliefs and feelings and notice what this reveals to you about yourself. Remind yourself of your aim to find true love and take steps to work through any resistance you might have had to enable you to give your-self permission to play. As always, if you think or sense you might need some professional support with this in order to help you to contact this part of yourself, do seek it.

Discover what your childlike self likes to do

You will not discover what makes your heart sing by think-ing, reasoning and using logic. Rather, you need to allow the childlike part of yourself to express itself and it will guide you to fun activities. In order to discern which part of you is guiding the actions you come up with, if it involves some-thing that could be described as an adult pursuit, such as drinking alcohol, shopping for clothes or taking drugs, it will be from the fearful part of you, the ego. If doing the activity makes you laugh (without any assistance from a chemical substance), particularly a real belly laugh, or if it makes you feel naturally carefree, even for a moment, then you are consciously connected to your Inner Child.

Exercise

Take a few deep breaths and allow yourself to think back for a moment to your childhood. Were you allowed to play and have fun? Were you encouraged to do so? If so, what did you enjoy doing? Do you still do any of those activities now? If you missed out in your childhood, what did you always want to do that you didn't do? What fun activity would you like to do now if you knew no-one was judging you for doing it? Allow your childlike self to have the fun it would have chosen. Is there a fun, childlike activity that you still do but that you would like to do more often?

Make a list of all these things and commit to making

space in your life to do something on a regular basis. You may like to start with one a week, or one a month, whatever feels appropriate for you. You may like to pair up with another person who is working through the book and share a childlike fun experience together.

It doesn't have to be anything expensive or spectacular. My Inner Child, for example, currently gets great joy out of skipping and dancing around the living room during my writing breaks while singing along at the top of my voice to 'Fly' by Hilary Duff!

Follow your passion and live your dream

In addition to committing to doing what makes your heart sing in your leisure time, you also have the innate ability to do what makes your heart sing in terms of a career. This is sometimes referred to as our 'life's purpose' or our vocation in life. The significant difference between a vocation and other work is that when you follow your passions and live your dream, you honour that childlike part of yourself and so it doesn't feel like work. You love what you do and would do it even if you didn't get paid, though of course it's an added bonus when you are rewarded financially. If you have financial challenges you may opt, as many people do, to keep your day job but invest some of your time in doing what makes your heart truly sing outside of work.

Exercise

Take a few minutes to reflect on what your passions are, on joyful things that make your heart sing. When you were asked as a child what you wanted to be when you grew up, what did you say? What thing(s) on the list do you wish today you could do? What do you dream about doing but put off because of time, money or lack of qualifications?

What would you do if you knew you could only succeed at it? What would you do if you had no fear of people rejecting you for doing it? Record your thoughts. Then, ask yourself how willing you are at the moment to take this further, to do whatever you need to in order to take one step forward in realising your dream. It might involve doing some research on the internet. You may like to contact your local adult education college. It might mean speaking to others who already do what you want to do. Allow yourself to explore, to be open to opportunities and have fun with it.

Keep your promises

Making your heart sing requires trust between your adult self and your childlike self – just as children in general need to be able to trust the adults around them in order to relax and have fun. When we have neglected or repressed aspects of ourselves previously, this can take time to develop. In order to make your heart sing, you have to take care of your childlike self in that if you make a promise to do something – to go ice skating next weekend, for example – you must commit to doing it no matter what. Therefore, only make the promises to your Inner Child that you are prepared to keep, in order to build a trusting relationship.

SECRET FIVE

Know what you want and ask for it

Do you know what you want?

If you are single, have you consciously thought about the qualities of The One? Do you know how you would like them to be aside from tall, dark and handsome (and rich perhaps!)? Do you know what true love means to you? What does it look like or feel like? Do you know how you want to be treated within your true love relationship when you find it? If you are in a relationship but are discontented, what qualities does The One for you have? What does true love mean to you? Do you know how you want to be treated in your true love relationship?

When we are single, we frequently know we don't want to date a particular kind of person, or someone of a certain profession, or with a certain accent, or of a certain height, weight or hair colour. We might focus on what we know we don't want to feel in our single state or with the next partner, such as lonely, rejected, unworthy and unlovable. We probably know that we don't want to be let down again. Hence, we carry the thoughts of what we *don't* want in our minds, focusing on the negative. Often, the only positive we focus on, what we know we *do* want, is to find someone who loves us, will stay with us, perhaps marry us, and/or possibly have a baby with us.

Equally, when we are discontented in our relationship we usually know that we don't want to continue feeling the way we do but we may not think about how we would really like to feel. Similarly, we probably don't think about how we would actually like to be treated by our partner. Rather, we often focus on what irritates us or what we would like to change about them instead.

Why do we find ourselves unclear about true love and trying to avoid what we don't want in our lives? One reason is that we may have grown up around adults who were less than loving towards themselves or their partner. They may have had the type of relationship that we decided from an early age we didn't want to emulate and so we spend our time trying not to do so. Another key reason is a lack of awareness. Unfortunately, the power of the unconscious mind is not taught to us in schools. So, until we actively work to enhance our self-awareness, for example by studying NLP, we do not consider this.

Nevertheless, our reality is a mirror of our own mind, reflecting to us what we have created with our conscious and unconscious thoughts. Because of the power of our thoughts, through knowing what we don't want in our lives and focusing on it we create exactly that – more of what we don't want! 'Whether it's a thought of something you want or a thought of something you don't want – your attention invites it into your experience' (p.41), confirm Esther and Jerry Hicks in *Ask and It Is Given*. This is exactly how the Universal Law of Attraction (which is discussed further in Secret Six) works too. Therefore, whether we are single or in a relationship, it is important to know what we really want with regard to true love and to keep our attention on that instead.

In addition, when we are asleep to our true selves our lives are dominated by our fearful self, in other words our ego. It encourages us to focus on externals, which, as previously mentioned, provide only short-term quick fixes and the illusion of happiness. Hence, if we focus on someone's looks, profession, material possessions or other external factors rather than their internal qualities, it leads us away from long-term happiness.

Getting what we want

Before we become more consciously aware, we are also naturally oblivious to the power of the Universe (or cosmos, as it is also referred to) to support us on our quest to find true love and The One. Our lack of awareness, and sometimes a reluctance to reach out for assistance, could have resulted in our missing out on another great opportunity to find what we want.

The Universe, though, has its own laws, such as the Universal Law of Attraction introduced earlier. These laws must be respected and adhered to if we are to benefit from them, just as in nature. If, for example, a gardener wishes to cultivate a plant in their garden, they will do all they can to ensure that it grows, such as planting the seed at the appropriate time of year, watering it regularly and feeding it, and so on. In this way the gardener demonstrates respect for the laws of nature and works in harmony with them to create their desire. When we work out what we want and ask for it in the way that the Universe requires, as explained in the 'How To' section, we work in harmony with it and are able to create true love in our lives.

Benefits of knowing what you want and asking for it

Receive help from the powerful universe

Although the more traditional methods of searching for true love, such as joining dating agencies, can assist us on the path to finding it, asking the Universe for support enhances our possibilities much more in ways that often seem magical, even miraculous. The Universe consists of energy which is everywhere and in all things, including people; this means it has a client 'database' which is universal and infinite. Consequently, it is the best and most powerful 'dating agency' on the planet!

Improved focus and clear direction

When I was younger, I hoped I would be married by the time I was 25 years old. It was a wish I had at the back of my mind. I didn't know what I wanted more specifically than this. Because I had little focus or direction I allowed myself to enter into encounters or relationships that would never help me achieve my wish. When we have only a vague notion of what we want, such as a partner or a better relationship, we are like a ship without a rudder, trying to travel in a particular direction without anything to keep us on course. In addition, because of the power of our unconscious mind and the way the Universal Law of Attraction works, when our thoughts are mainly on what is lacking in our lives we sabotage ourselves and our ability to create what we want.

This vagueness, coupled with a negative mindset, confuses the cosmos and renders it unable to assist us. In contrast, knowing what we want and asking for it changes our thoughts for the better, improves our focus and gives us clear direction. This greatly enhances our ability to reach our destination as we are starting to work in harmony with the Universal Law of Attraction and we're better equipped to make healthier choices for ourselves, ones which help us to remain on course. It also assists the process of discerning The Other and The One much more easily when they show up in our lives.

Speedier process of finding true love

Without knowing what we want, we frequently find ourselves settling for less, for unloving experiences or life with The Other. This slows down the process of creating what we want in our lives. When we know what we want, ask for it and remain focused, we are more likely to refuse to settle for that which is unlike true love, which amplifies the power of our request to the Universe and thus speeds up the process of finding true love.

A happier and more fulfilling life

When we know and really understand that we can create our own love and happiness, we give ourselves the opportunity to take positive action to achieve our desires. Taking responsibility, becoming aware of what we want and following it up with action is essential for happiness, as Nick Williams in *Powerful Beyond Measure* confirms: 'Knowing, living by and doing what we want, with integrity, is the greatest principle for a happy, powerful and fulfilled life' (p.72).

How to know what you want and ask for it

Take an inventory of your relationships

At this point, it is useful to observe your past relationship history along with your present situation. This can assist you in becoming consciously aware of what you want to avoid creating and what you'd like to experience in the future.

Exercise

You need to take an inventory of all your past and present relationship experiences in chronological order. Once you have the list, allow yourself to remember what you enjoyed and what you didn't like about each relationship (or what you consider to be the most significant ones if you have a long list of experiences!) and make a note of the information. Focus on how it began, what it was like in the middle and how it ended. Some questions you might like to ask yourself are: what were the key problems in the relationship? How did you perceive yourself in the relationship? What do you think or feel went wrong or changed? What did you want to be different? How did you feel about yourself in each relationship? What feelings did each relationship trigger in you? What fears were evoked in you during the relationship?

In addition, reflect on any periods when you were single in the past, and currently, if applicable. Was it a conscious choice to be single or do you believe it was forced upon you? What did (or do) you enjoy about being single? What did (or do) you dislike about it? What thoughts and feelings about yourself did (or does) being single evoke in you? Did you have any one-night stands or flings during that time? If so, how did it affect the perception of yourself? How did they make you feel about yourself? Were you hoping they would become something more or were you genuinely happy with the experience as it was? Make a note of this information too.

This information should then give you a better idea of what you want true love to look or feel like for you. Sometimes, however, it can be challenging to see the wood for the trees when we are so closely and emotionally connected with the information. Therefore, you might need to seek the support of your trusted friend or relative, or someone in the helping profession, to help you gain clarity.

Make a list of what you do not want

This may seem strange, given what has been said previously about negative thoughts and the Universal Law of Attraction. Nonetheless, as you work through the exercise it will become clearer that having a conscious awareness of what you don't want at this point in time can assist the process of finding true love.

Exercise

Using the information gained from your inventory and other knowledge you now have about yourself, make a list of what you *don't* want in The One or in a true love relationship. Do this whether you are single, casually dating or in a relationship as you will need it for the next exercise.

Transform the list into what you *do* want

Because of the way the Universal Law of Attraction works, in conjunction with the power of our unconscious mind to create what we focus our attention on in our lives, you now need to transform the list of what you don't want into what you *do* want.

Exercise

Taking the previous information, go through each item or quality on your list and write it in the affirmative. If, for example, you wrote 'I don't want someone who seems to be ashamed to be with me' you need to change it to something like 'I want to be with someone who is proud to be with me'. At the end of the process, review each item and ensure that it is in the affirmative.

Focus on internal qualities

As mentioned in the introduction to this Secret, when we focus on a person's looks, profession, material possessions or other external factors it leads us towards unhappiness. Therefore, for true love and happiness it is important to focus on internal qualities such as being kind, honest, loving and so on. Using your list of what you *do* want, complete the exercise below.

Exercise

Review your list. As you do so, notice where you might have included any external or ego-based characteristics of The One, such as hair or eye colour, or perhaps a particular body shape. That aside, it is my belief that it is part of a healthy, true love relationship to find our partner physically attractive. If you also believe this, you will need to specify that you want to be physically attracted to your partner. The Universe will take care of how this happens for you (see Secret Seven). Go through the list of what you want and ensure that it includes only internal qualities.

Remember the law of free will

You also need to ensure that your list excludes anything which goes against the Law of Free Will. This universal law means that you cannot force others to do something just because you want them to. You may want your current partner to alter their behaviour towards you. You may want an ex-partner to change their mind and take you back. Alternatively, you may be physically attracted to the new person at work and hoping, rather than knowing, that they are The One.

If this is what you believe or think you want, you are being dominated by your fearful ego rather than led by your spirit. Remind yourself that you cannot make other people change their thoughts, feelings or behaviours. You can only change your own. Allow yourself to trust that there is someone for you other than the ex-partner or any other person you have your eye on. This is why it is important to define the qualities you want and trust that the Universe will bring whoever matches that to you.

Exercise

Review your list and notice if you have written anything that involves another person's will, such as 'I want my partner to change', 'I want my ex to take me back', 'I want the new person at work to fall in love with me'. What is it that you want to change about your current partner? Dig deeper within yourself, look at what this triggers in you and see what you need to change within (or give to) yourself. If you think you want your ex back, what is it you believe this person will give you? What fears do you have around being single or finding someone new? Reflect on the underlying issues, remove the item from your list and write what you *would* want, if you totally trusted the process.

Sometimes, this can be such an entrenched pattern for us (i.e. always wanting your partner to change, turning to an ex, etc.) that we may need the support of someone in the helping profession to uncover the underlying issues and work through them.

Design a celestial advert

The Universe is ready, willing and able to support us, but we have to align ourselves with it by consciously asking for its help, as Esther and Jerry Hicks point out: 'without the asking that precedes it, there could be no answering' (p.35). So, once you are clear about what you want, you need to consciously ask the Universe for it by designing what I call a 'celestial advert'.

Exercise

Using the information from the list you created of what you *do* want, ensuring that all the items are in the affirmative, focused on internal qualities and so on, take a clean sheet of paper and write your celestial advert.

This time, you need to write it in the present tense because, for the Universe, only the present is real. Stating 'I want' in your celestial advert puts your request in the future, which does not exist for the Universe. Therefore, it will literally leave you wanting! Furthermore, by stating it in such a way that it reads as though the person is in your life already, it tells your unconscious mind that it is your reality. This enhances the creative process. So, you need to omit the word 'want' from your celestial advert. If you have written 'I want a partner who is kind, loving and compassionate. I want a partner with a good sense of humour' and so on, you now need to write 'My partner *is* kind, loving and compassionate. My partner *has* a good sense of humour' and so forth.

SECRET SIX

Become The One

How much are you like The One?

In Secret Five, we discovered how to receive support from the Universe by finding out what we want and asking for it with our celestial advert. If we are single, we may understandably expect that all we need to do now is to see if the people who appear in our lives match our advert. However, unless we consciously work on ourselves to heal the issues surrounding our unhappiness with being single or the problems that arose in our previous relationships, we will just attract more of the same through the Universal Law of Attraction. Therefore, we will either remain unhappily single, repelling potential partners on an unconscious level, or we will attract a new person who will trigger in us the same issues as before – hence it will appear that we have the misfortune to attract the wrong people.

Equally, if we are in a relationship, we might presume that we need only wait for our partner to miraculously become the person we described in our advert, or for another partner – The One – to appear in our lives, in order for us to find true love and happiness. But the Universal Law of Attraction does not support this either. This less traditional method of finding true love requires us to be proactive, and thus we must heed the words of Gandhi and 'be the change you want to see in the world'.

Some changes will have already occurred as we have been working through the other Secrets with regard to improving the relationship with ourselves. Nevertheless, if we are to be in harmony with the Universe and benefit from its powerful energy, we need to work to consciously become like the one we have asked for in our celestial advert. What does this mean?

In the physical world, the world of the conventional method of searching for true love externally, we find that opposites are frequently attracted to each other. On the other hand, when we search for true love using this less conventional method and co-create with the Universe using its laws, particularly the Universal Law of Attraction, we find that opposites do not attract. Rather, people who are alike are attracted to each other. Dr Wayne Dyer aptly explains this point and the significance of becoming The One in *The Power of Intention*: 'This is a universe of attraction and energy. You can't have a desire to attract a mate who's confident . . . and expect that desire to be manifested if you're thinking and acting in nonconfident . . . ways' (p.203).

Likewise, if in our celestial advert we state that The One for us is trusting and trustworthy yet we do not trust ourselves or have difficulty trusting other people, we are not being like that which we wish to attract. This is a Universe of attraction and energy, as the quote from Wayne Dyer states, and energy vibrates and attracts at different levels. Simply put, when we are depressed, our energy vibration is low and we attract people and situations to us that are also of a low energy. We will find ourselves struggling to create what we desire. In contrast, when we are happy, our energy vibration is high and we attract people and situations to us of a higher energy. We seem to be 'in the flow' and find it easier to create what we want in our lives. Thus, in order to benefit from the Universal Law of Attraction, to become a powerful 'celestial magnet' and attract to us what we desire, we need to resolve this or any other inner conflict and raise our energy vibration by aligning our thoughts, feelings and actions more with that which we wish to attract.

Furthermore, until we actively commit to becoming The One, we might not acknowledge or recognise within ourselves the qualities we have described in our celestial advert. Whether we are single or in a relationship, when we do not recognise and validate these qualities in ourselves, it affects our self-esteem and we perpetuate the cycle of co-dependency, seeking outside of ourselves what we perceive we lack. Similarly, when we do not see or feel the qualities in ourselves, and we do attract someone to us, that person will not recognise those qualities within themselves, because like attracts like. Therefore, we find that the person we attract is someone who is seeking in us what they believe they lack, hoping that this will make them feel complete and happy, and vice versa. Rather than having a healthy, loving relationship with themselves, this person could be described as 'needy'. They will be reflecting back to us our own neediness, which we may or may not consciously be aware of. So, we continue to cultivate co-dependent relationships with The Other instead of true love with The One.

In sum, due to the Universal Law of Attraction, the person we become has a direct influence on what we attract. Hence, if we still wish to find true love, we need to take this seemingly unconventional step of focusing inwards, resolving our internal conflicts and healing any other issues that may be blocking us, such as unforgiveness, in order that we can become The One for ourselves.

Benefits of becoming The One

Even better relationship with ourselves

The purpose of the Seven Secrets is to assist the process of transforming the relationship we have with ourselves from what may have been a less than loving, a neglectful, or even an abusive one, to a relationship that is nurturing, loving and considerate of all aspects of ourselves, mind, body and spirit. Becoming The One is a hugely significant aspect of this because, by consciously doing so, we bring any qualities previously hidden in our unconscious into our conscious awareness and validate them. In this way, we further enhance the benefits of the earlier Secrets. Subsequently, we find that we like ourselves even more and our sense of self-love (of our true self) increases. We become even more committed to being true to ourselves, ensuring that we have more fun in our lives and making our dreams happen. Consequently, we develop an even better relationship with ourselves and, in the process, we learn to liberate ourselves from co-dependency and find the true love we have been searching for.

Attract what we desire with less effort

Following on from the above, the other aim of the Seven Secrets is to assist us in finding The One, the partner for us. The celestial advert in Secret Five helps us to begin focusing our attention on this, but becoming The One enhances this process further. By consciously becoming like The One, as explained previously, we actively develop into a powerful celestial magnet, drawing to us that which we desire using the Universal Law of Attraction.

Because of the power of the Universe and its ability to transcend geographical and other potentially limiting factors, following this path seems to take less effort than the conventional methods of searching for true love. In other words, we can leave the 'how' we will meet The One for the Universe to deal with. This links to synchronicity, explained below. Furthermore, in my experience, the process of becoming The One is far more rewarding.

Enjoy synchronistic gifts

Some people are more comfortable choosing to believe in coincidences: these days, I am more comfortable believing in synchronicity. Moments of synchronicity, of things seemingly magically happening together, are signs that the Universe is assisting us, supporting us on our path towards whatever it is that we desire, including true love. When we consciously work to become The One, it demonstrates to the Universe that we are fully committed, mind, body and spirit, to finding true love in our lives. Subsequently, the Universe conspires to support us in every way, and thus we open ourselves up to experience the Universe's beautiful gifts of synchronicity.

These synchronicities, in my experience, illuminate the path to The One, and what some might perceive as miracles become everyday occurrences. These are the factors which I believe brought my husband and I together on the same NLP course in North London while I was living in South London and he was dividing his time between Wales and the south coast of England.

How to become The One

Release any resistance you might have

For some people this might seem like the least appealing secret! The part of us that is afraid might try to deceive us into believing that the conventional method of focusing externally, outside of ourselves, is easier. But we need to remind ourselves that what we have done before has not worked, otherwise we would not have picked up this book. In addition, a half-hearted attempt will not create for us the true love which we say we want to experience in our lives, because the Universe only supports focused commitment.

Exercise

Take a moment to review your celestial advert from Secret Five. As you read about The One you are asking for, and the qualities of your true love relationship, notice what your reaction is to doing what you would need to do to become The One yourself. Is there any resistance or reluctance on your part to work on yourself in this way? What do you believe would help you to be more willing or more committed to having this wonderful relationship with yourself? Or, are you already ready and willing to commit completely to the process now?

Notice what your observations, thoughts and feelings reveal about yourself in terms of your willingness at this time.

Discover what you need to work on

As you have worked through the other Secrets, you will have developed the skills and internal qualities to assist you in knowing yourself better. However, there is always more to learn about ourselves. Reviewing where you are now on your journey and identifying any persistent or unresolved issues will give you new insights that can help you in becoming The One.

Exercise

As you review each item in your celestial advert again, examine the relationship you currently have with yourself. What are you asking the cosmos for? Is it a person who is kind and loving? If so, ask yourself how kind and loving you currently are towards yourself. Have you requested someone who makes time for fun in their life? If so, examine how much time for fun you really make in your life. Have you asked for someone who is ready and able to commit to you? To what extent do you believe or feel you are ready and able to commit? And so forth.

Notice how closely you correspond to each of the items in your celestial advert, and be kind to yourself as you do so.

Acknowledge the qualities you do perceive in yourself

According to the Universal Law of Attraction, like attracts like. Therefore, if you are unhappily single or in a discontented relationship, it is important to increase your self-awareness even further and enhance what you think and how you feel about yourself. This next exercise involves consciously validating your own personal positive qualities.

Exercise

Using the information you obtained from the previous exercise, allow yourself to acknowledge the qualities from the advert that you are able to recognise in yourself at this point. As you do this, write down these points in a separate list using the following example: 'I am becoming kinder and more loving towards myself'; 'I make more time for fun now than I ever have'; 'I am very committed to myself' and so on.

Review your new list and, as you do so, allow yourself to get in touch with what it is like or how it feels to recognise these qualities within yourself. Allow yourself some time to see yourself being like the person you have described. Hear yourself being kind, loving and compassionate, for example. Take some time to feel yourself being this person and having this kind of relationship. Notice the images, thoughts, sounds or feelings this evokes in you as you connect with the qualities of The One and your true love experience.

Record your thoughts and feelings and review them regularly to remind yourself of how far you have come already, and also to help keep your thoughts and feelings focused on what you truly want.

Be the change you want to see

As mentioned earlier, you need to continue to 'be the change you want to see in the world'! Therefore, taking the qualities which you do not perceive in yourself at the moment, or those that you think or feel you could improve on (being less self-critical, kinder to self, etc.) or what you need to make more time for (perhaps having more fun or more relaxation), commit to making the changes that you need to in order to become The One.

Exercise

Using the list of qualities you believe you need to work on, write down the items that you think or feel confident you can work on by yourself using the knowledge you have gained from this book and other information you have. An example may be 'be more loving towards myself'.

Then write any other items that you believe you would benefit from having some assistance with, perhaps to discover an underlying issue that may be blocking you from perceiving this quality in yourself or to learn new behaviour. When you have completed this list, take steps to seek the support that you need (see Further Reading and Other Resources). You can also seek the support of your trustworthy friend, helping professional and so forth. Again, while you are addressing these issues, rather than using this as an excuse to berate yourself, you need to continue to be as compassionate as possible towards yourself. Once more, congratulate yourself on how far you've come!

SECRET SEVEN

Let go

The final challenge

If you are single, is there a part of you that likes your life the way it is? Are you reluctant to change it, or afraid of it being altered in some way? Is there an aspect of you that fears losing your independence? Deep down, do you have a fear of intimacy? Do you still have an emotional reaction when you receive news of others settling down and getting married? When you go on a date, how much do you think about a future with the person and hope it will lead to a relationship? How impatient are you to find The One? Would you be upset, as I was, if a psychic were to tell you it would be another six months, or longer, before you meet that special someone?

If you are in a relationship but are discontented, how attached are you to your partner? How much do you want them to be The One? Are you staying with them in the hope that things will return to how they were when you first got together? Are you convincing yourself your partner will change and become The One? How attached are you to being in control and trying to make this happen? Do you have friends in common? Do you own a property or a pet together? Are you afraid you'll lose your social life, your friends, the roof over your head or a cherished pet if you leave the relationship or if your partner leaves you? How much could your attachment to the aforementioned be leading you to stay in the relationship?

While these concerns and feelings are very common and understandable, when we have chosen to raise our conscious awareness and find true love and The One using the less conventional method described in this book, we cannot allow ourselves to remain attached in this way. As Mike George explains in *In the Light of Meditation*: 'attachment is the root of fear and fear and love cannot co-exist' (p.57). In other words, attachment equals fear. When we are attached, and thus in fear, we find ourselves trying to control everyone and everything around us. Therefore, we must let go of our attachments and our habit of trying to control in order to free ourselves from co-dependence and find true love.

Recognising when we have not let go

When we are attached to a specific outcome, certain people or possessions and so on, we are at that moment seeing life through our fearful 'false' self. This aspect of us perceives these situations, people or things as giving us a sense of security, love and happiness. As we know, though, this is an illusion. It may lead to very brief moments of happiness, but because they are aspects of co-dependency rather than true love, it leads us away from our true self and thus results in suffering.

The most common forms of fear are 'worry, anxiety and tension' (p.57), according to Mike George. Therefore, we are able to recognise that we have not let go when we are worried, anxious or tense. Instead, we are attached to something, someone or life being a certain way. Similarly, we can recognise that we have not let go when we experience anger, frustration, disappointment, resistance, impatience, inflexibility, non-acceptance or jealousy, or if we are clinging, or if we find ourselves constantly thinking about a certain person and seem to be unable to stop thinking about them.

When we accept an invitation to a party, a dinner, a wedding or any other event, desperately hoping that The One might be there (whether we are single or in a discontented relationship), we are emotionally attached. Being afraid to turn down an invitation in case we miss the opportunity to meet The One, or accepting solely in the hope they might be there rather than because we would love to go, is a sign of emotional attachment. When getting ready for the event, if we find ourselves being overly anxious about our appearance, deciding what to wear with the purpose of attracting someone, or in the hope that our current partner will improve their behaviour towards us, we have not let go.

On arrival at the event, if we find ourselves looking around the room desperately hoping to spot The One, we have not let go. If at the end of the event we leave feeling disappointed, lonely, rejected or fearful because The One was not there, or because our current partner did not treat us as we wanted them to, we have not let go.

Recognising when we have let go

Letting go, on the other hand, looks, sounds and feels very different. When we practise detachment and are able to let go, we release the fears and all the uncomfortable feelings that went with it. Rather, we allow ourselves to experience inner peace and joy. Furthermore, we can recognise we have let go when we are trusting, flexible, open, calm, relaxed, patient, accepting, allowing, grateful, satisfied and are able to go with the flow. When we have let go, we are able to trust that the Universe is supporting us and know that everything happens for a reason. We are able to trust this less conventional process of finding true love and happiness.

When we are single and have let go, we are detached emotionally from the outcome of a date and enjoy the date for what it is in the moment. We are relaxed as to whether the person asks us on another date or not. We are calm if they do and if they don't. We are open to when The One appears in our life and are patient, trusting in the Universe's timing. We keep our focus on continuing to become The One and making our hearts sing. We are able to leave many things up to the Universe: not only the 'when' The One shows up in our lives but also the 'how' and what they look like. Furthermore, we enjoy learning more about ourselves from each dating experience and from the period when we are not dating. Whether we have many dates or none, our relationship with ourselves and our happiness are unaffected.

Likewise, when we are in a relationship and have let go, our focus shifts from trying to decide whether our current partner is The One or not, to becoming The One for us ourselves. By releasing the need to know, we allow ourselves to connect with our intuition, which gives us this information. Thus, we are relaxed about whether we choose to remain in our current relationship or leave. When we let go, we release the need to try and control our partner, to try and make them act as we want them to, or to stay in the relationship. Instead, we are able to allow them to be themselves and know that if they decide they no longer wish to be with us, then that is OK. Rather than fight it, we are able to go with the flow and face it with courage as we trust that the Universe is supporting us. Whether our relationship circumstances change or not, our love for ourselves and our happiness are unaffected.

Continuing the example of accepting an invitation, if we are in a relationship and have let go, we can accept an invitation for purposes other than the possibility of meeting The One. We are calm and relaxed about whether or not they are there. When we are getting ready, we are relaxed about our appearance and focus on dressing to please ourselves. At the event, we might have a look around the room out of curiosity to see who is there, free from emotional attachment. If we go with our current partner, we are able to observe how they are behaving towards us, without reacting emotionally. Equally, we might observe who else is there, but we have no emotional need to seek out someone else to pay us some attention. We are able to control our emotions, remember who we truly are, go with the flow and enjoy the experience for its own sake.

In summary, in Secret Five, by formulating what we want and asking for it, we sent a clear message to the Universe and consciously allowed our true self to guide us in our quest. In Secret Six, by working towards becoming The One ourselves, we ensure that our message to the Universe is a committed and congruent one, which enables us to magnetically attract to us what we want. Now, in Secret Seven, we are required to let go of our attachment to having our celestial advert answered. By doing so, paradoxically, we allow it to happen! This works with the Universal Law of Detachment, meaning that we can know what we want, ask for it and work to become The One, but if we want it so badly that we are attached to the result, it lowers our vibes. Subsequently, this acts like an energy shield around us and blocks the magnetic pull. Thus our desire cannot reach us. Again, only our true self, which is aligned with the Universe and knows only love, can lead us to true love and real happiness.

Benefits of letting go

Enhanced possibility of attracting the one

All the other Secrets assist the process of finding true love and The One, but unless we are able to let go, we create a block to true love, as previously explained. Therefore, by detaching from the outcome of our celestial advert and letting go, we enhance the possibility of attracting The One to us in this lifetime.

Greater self-acceptance

Nevertheless, when we have found true love within ourselves (being aware that we may have days when we feel strongly connected to our true self and thus feel more love for ourselves, and other days when we pay more attention to our fearful false self and thus feel less loving towards ourselves) we have no emotional reaction to the possibility that we may not be destined to be with The One in this lifetime. We are no longer needy and co-dependent. Instead, we feel whole and complete and experience inner peace. This is not a false layer of positivity; rather it is a deep knowing that we are all right as we are, perfectly lovable, loved, loving and complete in our own right. Letting go, therefore, enables us to experience greater self-acceptance.

Relationship issues solved more easily

Mike George points out that our attachments 'not only drain the energy of our consciousness, they will, over time, poison our relationships' (p.57). Hence, if we are currently in a relationship and allow ourselves to let go as described, we find either that our relationship naturally improves as a consequence, or that letting go will enable us to move on from the relationship (if that is what our intuition has been guiding us to do). Alternatively, when we stop clinging on and being controlling, we might find that our partner chooses to leave the relationship, which also means that our relationship issues are solved more easily. In this way, we continue to free ourselves from co-dependency and allow space for The One to come into our lives.

How to let go

Be attentive to yourself

Letting go takes not only the self-discipline and willpower needed to break old habits and create new ones. It also requires an even greater level of self-awareness. The more we pay attention to our thoughts, our patterns, our behaviours and so on, the more we empower ourselves to change and make the choice to let go.

Exercise

Whether you are single or in a relationship, allow yourself a few moments to notice the thoughts, images, sounds or feelings that come up for you when you contemplate making the choice to let go. What happens when you contemplate letting go of finding true love and The One and welcome uncertainty, as described in this Secret? Notice whether you have any resistance to letting go. If so, ask yourself what it would take, or what you would need, for you to make the choice to let go. Reflect, without judgement, on where you are now on your journey with regard to this aspect.

Make space in your life

Letting go involves making space for yourself and The One in your life. If you were really honest with yourself, could you say that you make yourself very busy, not only with work projects but also in your leisure time, in an attempt to avoid uncomfortable feelings such as loneliness? If so, you will need to process this and any other underlying issue to enable yourself to create more balance in your life. An aspect of this includes spending some time in quiet reflection. Although it is important to spend time with family and friends and to socialise, it is equally important to make space in your life to nurture yourself and allow for The One. Each person intuitively knows with experience what the right balance is for them, and so allow yourself to experiment and monitor how you feel as you progress.

Heal your fears

Following on from the previous point, it may seem challenging to let go of hoping that our ex-partner will take us back, or to leave an unhappy relationship because we may still perceive the other person as our source of love. In addition, being in a relationship or going from one encounter to the next can act like a temporary plaster over our emotional wounds. However, as explained in Secret Two, the love that we seek outside of ourselves is always within us. It is our conscious awareness of this love that becomes obscured by these emotional blocks.

Exercise

Using the information you obtained from the previous exercises, in addition to other information you have become aware of regarding any remaining blocks to love and letting go, allow yourself to make the commitment to resolve these issues. If you believe you would benefit from professional help to work through any remaining issues then do seek it.

Change your habits

In order to let go, you need to change your habits, such as an old habit of actively looking for The One. This takes awareness and tenacity. Think of it as re-training yourself so that instead of looking for The One, you focus on yourself and developing the qualities of The One as described in your celestial advert. You need to become even more aware of your thoughts, your emotions and your habits, particularly in terms of when or where you might find yourself actively looking for The One.

Allow yourself to focus on creating fun and fulfilment in your life by accepting invitations, attending new classes or even speed dating nights, with the intention of having fun and meeting new people, rather than of finding The One. Commit to discovering your passions and making time to nurture them. Breaking old habits and forming new behaviours takes consistent effort and patience. Therefore, as with giving up any habit, allow yourself to keep focused on the benefits of your new behaviour and give yourself regular healthy, nurturing rewards. You may also like to explore the subject of NLP to help with this.

Meditate regularly

Similarly, in order to break a habit, something else we need to learn is to control our thoughts and emotions. A good way to do this is by meditating on a regular basis. The more you meditate, the more you are able to observe your thoughts and emotions and thus enhance your ability to control them, rather than vice versa. As mentioned in Secret One, meditation is best practised at the same time on a daily basis. The more you practise, the easier it becomes as it forms a habit.

Exercise

If you have yet to begin to meditate, examine what might have been stopping you until now. Has it been that you are unsure how to do it? Or have you had a fear of not doing it right? Have you tried a few times and then given up? Could it be that you believe your mind is too busy to meditate? Or could you be making a lack of time an excuse? Whatever your reasons, if you still want to find true love, you need to take action to overcome the reasons that you allowed yourself not to do it in the past. So, find a local meditation class (see Other Resources) or read a book on meditation (see Further Reading). Examine your schedule and prioritise your commitments to allow you to find ten minutes to meditate every day.

Write it down

In my experience, written expression of our thoughts and feelings also assists the process of forming new habits.

Exercise

If you ever have the temptation to phone an ex-partner (when there is no practical reason for doing so), or perhaps find yourself obsessing about someone, or are anxious about being left on the shelf, write about it in your notepad or journal. Keep writing until you believe that you have written down, vented, or described, all your thoughts, images and feelings regarding this issue for you at this time. When you have finished writing (and you will know intuitively when to stop), allow yourself to reflect on what you have written so that you can understand what is really going on for you currently.

If this happens more than once, reflect on your journal entries and allow yourself to notice any patterns that recur. Notice whether your challenge with letting go coincides with anything in particular: for example, stressful work periods or emotional challenges with colleagues or friends, or even with PMT. Identify what your triggers are and use the information to help you strengthen your resolve to let go.

Have faith

Finally, letting go also involves having faith. To assist the process it can help to perceive yourself as having 'faith muscles'. When we first embark on an inner journey, our 'faith muscles' are often out of shape and, like other muscles, they need to be strengthened. Nevertheless, over time, with regular exercise in the form of the letting-go practices combined with a healthy diet of positive, loving thoughts, words and actions, these 'muscles' will become stronger. Consequently, because you will have formed a new habit of letting go, having faith in yourself will now be easier.

Conclusion

Now that you have read through the Seven Secrets, irrespective of whether you are single or in a relationship, you will have begun to understand what true love means for you. In completing the exercises within each Secret you will find that you enhance your clarity and understanding even further.

In addition, as you work through the exercises and live the Seven Secrets, you will discover that your self-awareness and your self-esteem increase along with your ability to be your true, authentic self. You will notice how your relationships are beginning to improve and how you are experiencing moments of pure joy more frequently than before.

As you progress on your journey, developing a healthier, more loving and nurturing relationship with yourself, the most important person in your life, you will begin to liberate yourself from co-dependency and find it easier to discern The One from The Other. You will also start to consciously experience the benefits of working with the infinite Universe, which is there to support you in creating your heartfelt desires.

It is important, as you do the exercises, to be kind to yourself and go at your own pace. You will need to be willing, flexible and creative so that you can make time for yourself. You might also want to remind yourself of your goal so that you can find it easier to continue along your path.

Finally, remember to praise yourself regularly for doing more than the average person to create the life that you desire, and before you know it, you will have found the love that you were looking for all along.

Bibliography

Bays, Brandon. *The Journey®: An Extraordinary Guide for Healing Your Life and Setting Yourself Free.* (Thorsons, 1999)

Bradshaw, John. *Home Coming: Reclaiming & Championing Your Inner Child.* (Piatkus, 1990)

Choquette, Sonia, PhD. *Trust Your Vibes: Secret Tools for Six-Sensory Living.* (Hay House Publishing, 2004)

Doyle, Laura. *The Surrendered Single.* (Simon & Schuster UK Ltd, 2002)

Dyer, Dr Wayne W. *Pulling Your Own Strings: How to Take Control of Your Life.* (Arrow Books, 2004. Quote reprinted by permission of The Random House Group)

Dyer, Dr Wayne W. *The Power of Intention.* (Hay House Publishing, 2004)

George, Mike. *In the Light of Meditation: A Guide to Meditation and Spiritual Development.* (O Books, 2004)

Hay, Louise L. *How to Heal Your Life.* (Hay House Publishing, 1999)

Hay, Louise L. *Life! Reflections on Your Journey.* (Hay House Publishing, 1995)

Hicks, Esther and Jerry. *Ask and It Is Given: Learning to Manifest Your Desires.* (Hay House Publishing, 2005)

Howard, Alex. *Why ME? My Journey from M.E. to Health & Happiness.* (Roximillion Publications: a division of Red Cherry Books)

Myss, Caroline, PhD. *Anatomy of the Spirit: The Seven Stages of Power and Healing.* (Bantam Books, 1997. Quote reprinted by permission of The Random House Group)

Tipping, Colin C. *Radical Forgiveness: Making Room for the Miracle.* (Global 13 Publications Inc., 2002)

Virtue, Dr Doreen. *Healing with the Angels: How the Angels can Assist You in Every Area of Your Life*. (Hay House Publishing, 1999)

Williams, Nick. *Powerful Beyond Measure: An Inspiring Guide to Personal Freedom*. (Transworld Publishers, 2003. Quote reprinted by permission of The Random House Group)

Further reading

In addition to the books listed in the bibliography, the following may also be useful:

Mind and emotions

Andreas, Steve and Faulkner, Charles. *NLP: The New Technology of Achievement*. (Nicholas Brealey Publishing, 1996)

Dyer, Dr Wayne. *You'll See It When You Believe It: The Way to Your Personal Transformation*. (Arrow Books Ltd, 1990)

Forward, Dr Susan with Buck, Craig. *Toxic Parents: Overcoming Their Hurtful Legacy and Reclaiming Your Life*. (Bantam Books, 1990)

Jampolsky, Gerald G. *Forgiveness: The Greatest Healer of All*. (Beyond Words Publishing, 1999)

Powell, John. *Why Am I Afraid to Tell You Who I Am?* (Fount Paperbacks/HarperCollins, 1995)

Body

Courteney, Hazel and Briffa, Dr John. *What's The Alternative?* (Boxtree, 1996)

Holford, Patrick. *The Optimum Nutrition Bible*. (Piatkus, 2002)

Kenton, Leslie. *The Power House Diet: The High-Raw, Low-Grain Miracle for Radiant Health, Good Looks and a Great Body*. (Vermillion London, 2004)

The Sivananda Yoga Vedanta Centre. *Learn Yoga in a Weekend*. (Dorling Kindersley Limited, 1993)

Spirit

Anderton, Bill. *A Piatkus Guide: Meditation*. (Piatkus Books, 1999)

Horan, Paula. *Empowerment Through Reiki: The Path to Personal and Global Transformation*. (Lotus Light Publications, 1998)

Thich Nhat Hanh. *The Miracle of Mindfulness: A Manual on Meditation*. (Beacon Press, 1987)

Virtue, Dr Doreen. *The Lightworker's Way: Awakening Your Spiritual Power to Know and Heal*. (Hay House Publishing, 1997)

Walsch, Neale Donald. *Conversations with God Book One: An Uncommon Dialogue*. (Hodder & Stoughton, 1995)

Whiteaker, Stafford. *The Good Retreat Guide*. (Rider, 2004)

Others

Capacchione, Lucia, PhD. *The Power of Your Other Hand*. (Newcastle Pub. Co. Inc., 1988)

Dilts, Robert, Hallbom, Tim and Smith, Suzi. *Beliefs: Pathways to Health & Well-Being*. (Metamorphous Press, 1990)

Riso, Don Richard and Hudson, Russ. *The Wisdom of the Enneagram: The Complete Guide to Psychological and Spiritual Growth for the Nine Personality Types*. (Bantam Books, 1999)

Williams, Nick. *The Work We Were Born to Do: Find the Work You Love, Love the Work You Do*. (Element Books Ltd, 1999)

Other resources

Alternatives (for inspiring talks and workshops)
St James's Church
197 Piccadilly
London, W1J 9LL
Tel: 020 7282 6711
www.alternatives.org.uk

Hoffman Institute UK (for the Hoffman Process)
Box 72 Quay House
River Road
Arundel
Sussex, BN18 9DF
Tel: 0800 0687114
www.hoffmaninstitute.co.uk

The Optimum Health Clinic (for nutrition, NLP training and consultations)
1 Harley Street
London, W1G 9QD
Tel: 0845 226 1762
www.theoptimumhealthclinic.com

The British Wheel of Yoga
BWY Central Office
25 Jermyn Street
Sleaford
Lincolnshire, NG34 7RU
Tel: 01529 306851
www.bwy.org.uk

UK Reiki Federation
PO Box 71
Andover
SP11 9WQ
Tel: 0870 850 2209
www.reikifed.co.uk

ANLP International (for NLP practitioners and training)
www.anlp.org

UKCP (United Kingdom Council for Psychotherapy)
www.ukcp.org.uk

Centre for Counselling and Psychotherapy Education (UKCP member organisation specialising in transpersonal therapy)
www.ccpe.org.uk

Brahma Kumaris World Spiritual University (for free courses on meditation, positive thinking and self-esteem)
Centres throughout the UK
www.bkwsu.com

About the author

Catherine Buchan BSc (Hons) is an experienced teacher and psychological coach. She holds a degree in Psychology and Counselling from the University of Surrey Roehampton. She is also a qualified Clinical Hypnotherapist and NLP practitioner.

Catherine is passionate about teaching others how to live conscious, authentic, empowered and happy lives and find true love. In addition, she is committed to continuously working on herself, enhancing her own self-awareness, authenticity, well-being and happiness.

For further information visit:-

www.catherinebuchan.com.